PROJECT ACHIEVEMENT

W9-BQU-102

George D. Spache, Ph.D.
Spache Educational Consultants

Evelyn B. Spache, Ed.D.
Spache Educational Consultants

And the Scholastic Editors

📖 SCHOLASTIC INC.

The Project Achievement Staff

Curriculum Consultant: Leonore K. Itzkowitz, Reading Specialist, New Jersey Public Schools
Editorial Director: Eleanor Angeles
Design: Taurins Design Associates
Photo Research: Sybille Millard

Revision Production Team: Rosalie Shagwert Hayek, Alexander Sinclair, Suzanne Sayegh Thomas

Art Credits: Andrea Baruffi, pp. 57, 81, 82, 94, 95, 102, 103 • Gwen Brodkin, pp. 20-21, 58-59 • Cynthia Watts Clark, pp. 80, 128 • Doris Ettlinger, pp. 44-45, 92, 104, 136-137 • Scott Pollack, pp. 113, 115, 130, 141 • Bill Purdom, pp. 23, 62-63, 100 • David Tamura, pp. 16-17, 40-41, 64-65, 112 • Katrina Taylor, pp. 15, 72-73

Cover Illustration: Jeanette Adams

Photo Credits: Courtesy of Bike Information Bureau, p. 5 • Scholastic Awards/Matt Rosenfeld, p. 7; Roy Jansen, p. 28; Jay Thornton, p. 30; Paul Margolies, p. 50; Brian Parks, p. 79 • Richard Lisman, left p. 140; Don Haisler, right p. 140; Ken Schatz, p. 149; Monte Paulsen, p. 197 • United Press International Photo, pp. 8, 49, 69, 71, 142 • Animals Animals/Leonard Lee Rue, III, p. 10; B. Smith, p. 61 • Courtesy of the Library of Congress, p. 12 • Arthur Tress, p. 19 • U.S. Coast Guard, p. 32 • James Gilmour, pp. 34-35, 84, 174, 175, 176, 178, 188, 190, 192 • AP/Wide World Photos, pp. 37, 112 • The Granger Collection, p. 39 • Courtesy of the Australian News and Information Bureau/W. Hartley, p. 43 • Howard Millard, p. 52 • Courtesy of Unimation, Inc., p. 54 • Canadian Pacific Airlines, p. 67 • Courtesy of the American Museum of Natural History/Charles H. Coles, p. 97 • Chase Money Museum, p. 107 • Wide World Photos, p. 114 • Classic Baseball Cards/Bert Randolph Sugar, 1977, Dover Publications, NY, pp. 116-117

Contents

Introduction 5

UNIT I
READING COMPREHENSION _____ 7

Part 1   Details 8
Lessons 1–7 10–23
Taking Tests 24

Part 2   Main Idea 28
Lessons 1–8 30–45
Taking Tests 46

Part 3   Inference 50
Lessons 1–12 52–75
Taking Tests 76

UNIT II
VOCABULARY _____ 79

Part 1   Words and Meaning 80
Words with the Same Meaning 81
Lessons 1–5 84–93
Words with Opposite Meanings 94
Lessons 6–8 96–101
Words That Sound Alike 102
Lessons 9–10 104–107
Taking Tests 108

Part 2   Context Clues 112
Lessons 1–5 116–125
Taking Tests 126

Part 3   Words with Several Meanings 128
Lessons 1–3 132–137
Taking Tests 138

Part 4   Word Parts 140
Lessons 1–2 144–147
Taking Tests 148

UNIT III
STUDY SKILLS ——————————————————— 149

Part 1   Visual Materials   150
Lesson 1   Map Reading   152
Lesson 2   Using a Compass Rose   154
Lesson 3   Using Symbols in a Map Key   156
Lesson 4   Finding Information on a Calendar   158
Lesson 5   Using a Table   160
Lesson 6   Getting Information from a Table .   162
Lesson 7   Using Symbols in a Pictograph . . .   164
Lesson 8   Understanding a Bar Graph   166
Lesson 9   Understanding a Line Graph   168
Lesson 10 Reading a Pie Graph   170
Taking Tests   172

Part 2   Reference Skills   174
Lesson 1   Alphabetical Order   176
Lesson 2   Using Guide Words in a Dictionary   178
Lesson 3   Reading Dictionary Entries   180
Lesson 4   Using a Table of Contents   182
Lesson 5   Using an Index   184
Lesson 6   Using Card Catalogs   186
Lesson 7   Choosing a Reference   188
Lesson 8   Using an Encyclopedia   190
Lesson 9   Choosing the Right Reference   192
Taking Tests   194

UNIT IV
TESTS ——————————————————————— 197

Test 1   Reading Comprehension   198
             Vocabulary   202
             Study Skills   205

Test 2   Reading Comprehension   208
             Vocabulary   212
             Study Skills   215
Vocabulary Glossary   218
Answer Key   221

Introduction

Everyone wants to read well. There is no secret about becoming a good reader. You have to practice. You can learn to read well by practicing four different ways:

1. **By following the ideas in a story.**

   Here is part of a story you will find in this book.

   Could you ride a bike with no pedals? The first bikes had wheels and handlebars. They had no pedals. You had to push your feet along the ground.

   In 1839, a man from Scotland attached pedals to a bike. He rode along a street, grinning and waving. Suddenly, he knocked over a small child. People remembered him for two things. He produced the first bike with pedals. He also caused the first bike accident.

   Finish the sentence. The first bikes had wheels but no __.

2. **By figuring out what new words mean.**

   The words under **A** are from the story above.
   Match each word with its meaning under **B**.

A	B
attached	smiling
grinning	made
produced	put on

Find out two more ways to read well on the next page.

3. **By using lists of facts and other visual materials.**

Use the table to answer the question below.

WHICH SIZE BIKE FOR YOU?

Length of Leg	Bike Frame
24 – 29 inches	17 inches
27 – 32 inches	20 inches
30 – 35 inches	23 inches
32 – 37 inches	25 inches

If your leg is 26 inches, what is the right size bike for you? __

4. **By knowing how to take reading tests.**

Ride a bike on the right, with the traffic. Pay attention to traffic lights and signs. Watch the traffic carefully. Day or night, drivers can't always see a bike very well.

Choose the best answer.

This paragraph is mostly about __.
   a. riding a bike at night
   b. riding a bike in traffic
   c. lights on a bike
   d. new traffic signs

Now you have practiced four kinds of reading skills. You will find the same kinds of skills in the rest of this book.

Answers to exercises: 1. pedals, **2.** attached-put on, grinning-smiling, produced-made, **3.** 17 inches, **4.** b

UNIT I
READING
COMPREHENSION

PART 1: *Details*   8

PART 2: *Main Idea*   28

PART 3: *Inference*   50

8

Details are the small parts in a whole thing. Study the picture on page 8. The picture shows a steelworker in a big city. There are many details in the picture. The following questions ask about some of these details.

Choose the best answer for each question.

1. Where is the man in the picture working?
   a. under a building
   b. on a street
   c. high above a city

Check your answer. Look back at the picture. Most of the buildings are below the worker. The right answer is **c**.

2. The worker is wearing ___.
   a. a baseball cap
   b. a hard hat
   c. a cowboy hat

Check your answer. Look at the worker's hat. Then choose the right detail. The answer is **b**.

3. The city in the picture is ___.
   a. near the water
   b. near a mountain
   c. near a park

Check your answer. Find the body of water and the bridge at the top of the picture. The right answer is **a**.

4. What part of the steelworker's building is in the picture?
   a. the front of the building
   b. only the tower
   c. only a steel beam

Check your answer. The only part of the building that is showing is a steel beam. The answer is **c**.

5. The building at the top of the picture is ___.
   a. being painted
   b. not yet finished
   c. falling down

Check your answer. Notice the open spaces in the building at the top of the picture. The building is not yet finished. The answer is **b**.

LESSON 1

Details are the small facts in a story. Read this story and look for the details. Finding details will help you understand what you read.

The Most Dangerous Animal

What is the most dangerous animal in the world? A bull is dangerous. A tiger is dangerous. A king cobra snake is dangerous, too. But one animal is stronger and meaner than any of these. It is the black buffalo of South Africa. The black buffalo may be the most dangerous animal in the world.

A black buffalo has a large head and horns as strong as steel. He will attack any living thing. It is a good idea to get out of his way quickly. The black buffalo has killed more hunters than any other animal.

Choose the best answer for each question.

1. A bull is a __ animal.
   a. small
   b. dangerous
   c. young

Check your answer. You may know the answer right away. If you are not sure of the answer, look back at the story on page 10. The story says a bull is *dangerous*. The answer is **b.**

2. Where does the black buffalo live?
   a. in South America
   b. in South Africa
   c. in the whole world

Check your answer. Before you choose one answer, read *all* the answers. *South America* and *South Africa* start with the same word. Look back at the story to find the word *South*. The right answer is **b.**

3. A black buffalo has __.
   a. a small head
   b. brown fur
   c. horns as strong as steel

Check your answer. Choose the right detail to finish the sentence. You will find the right words in the second paragraph of the story. The answer is **c.**

4. The black buffalo will attack any __ thing.
   a. living
   b. funny
   c. strong

Check your answer. In this question, a word is left out of a sentence. Look back at the story and find a sentence that is almost the same. Then find the missing word. The answer is **a.**

5. The black buffalo has killed __.
   a. tigers
   b. king cobra snakes
   c. hunters

Check your answer. Find a sentence like this one near the end of the story. Choose the right word. The answer is **c.**

Details in this story are about people, places, and numbers. Read the story and look for these details.

Bikes, Old and New

Could you ride a bike with no pedals? The first bikes had wheels and handlebars. They had no pedals. You had to push your feet along the ground. It wasn't much like riding at all.

In 1839, a man from Scotland put pedals on a bike. He rode along the street, smiling and waving. Suddenly, he knocked over a small child. People remembered him for two things. He built the first bike with pedals. He also caused the first bike accident.

Today, all bikes have pedals. Two popular types are the dirt bike used for hills and dirt roads, and the ten-speed bike used for long rides. There are also one-wheel bikes and bikes with many seats. In 1967, Jeff Killburn of England built one of the longest bikes for himself and 13 friends.

Choose the best answer for each question.

1. The first bikes had no ___.
   a. wheels
   b. pedals
   c. horns

2. Bikes had pedals after ___.
   a. 1800
   b. 1839
   c. 1967

3. Who caused the first bike accident?
   a. a man from Scotland
   b. Jeff Killburn
   c. a grandmother

4. The story says that a popular bike today has ___ speeds.
   a. 2
   b. 10
   c. 5

5. How many people can ride on one long bike in England?
   a. 13
   b. 14
   c. 20

Check your answers.

Question 1: Look for the right detail in the beginning of the story. The word *wheels* is in the story. But it is not the right answer. The answer is **b**.

Question 2: Look for dates in the story. Find the right one. The answer is **b**.

Question 3: To answer a question that starts with *who*, look for a name, or words about a person. The answer is **a**.

Question 4: Look for the right detail at the end of the story. The answer is **b**.

Question 5: The number 13 is in the story, but it is not the right answer. You have to count Jeff and his 13 friends. The answer is **b**.

Practice finding details in the next stories. Look back at each story to answer the five questions that follow it.

A Strange Sight

It was a cold morning on a beach in Florida. Only a few people were out. They came upon a strange sight. Huge black whales were lying on the sand. The whales were 20 feet long. They almost covered the beach.

Many of the whales were still alive. A rescue team came with boats and long ropes. They tied the ropes around the tails of some whales. They used the boats to pull the whales into deep water. Some of the whales turned around as soon as they were free. They began to swim back to the beach. About 50 whales were saved, but the others died on the beach.

Why did the whales swim onto the beach in the first place? They may have been following a leader. Whales swim in a group behind one old whale. The old whale in this group could have been sick. Sometimes a sick whale swims onto a beach.

Choose the best answer for each question.

1. The whales on the beach were in ___.
   a. Florida
   b. boats
   c. deep water

2. The rescue team tied ropes around the ___ of some whales.
   a. noses
   b. heads
   c. tails

3. What did some whales do after they were free?
   a. They went back to the beach.
   b. They pulled the ropes.
   c. They went into the boats.

4. How many whales were saved?
   a. 20
   b. about 50
   c. about 100

5. The story says that whales swim behind ___.
    a. a baby whale
    b. an old whale
    c. a boat

A Long Fall

Annie Taylor decided to try a dangerous stunt. She would go over a waterfall in a barrel. She would try this stunt at Niagara Falls. It is one of the highest waterfalls in the United States.

Annie Taylor was a teacher from Michigan. She knew that many people had tried this stunt. Most of them had given up. On October 24, 1901, Annie got ready to climb into a barrel. The barrel was heavy. It had seven iron rings around it and weighed 160 pounds. An iron block was tied to the bottom of the barrel so the barrel would not turn over.

Annie waved to a big crowd of people. "We'll meet again," she cried. "I won't say good-bye because I'm coming back."

The barrel began to move in the water. It splashed over the top of the waterfall. It dropped more than 150 feet straight down. All this time, Annie was strapped inside. The barrel hit bottom. It bounced away from the waterfall. Annie's friends got hold of the barrel and helped her out.

Annie was glad to be safe. She had a secret. She hadn't told anyone. Annie Taylor didn't know how to swim.

16

Choose the best answer for each question.

1. Annie Taylor was a __.
   a. swimmer
   b. climber
   c. teacher

2. Where did Annie do her stunt?
   a. at Niagara Falls
   b. in Michigan
   c. in the air

3. How much did the barrel weigh?
   a. 100 pounds
   b. 150 pounds
   c. 160 pounds

4. The barrel splashed over the top of the waterfall and __.
   a. stopped
   b. dropped straight down
   c. opened

5. Annie Taylor's secret was that she __.
   a. couldn't move
   b. couldn't wave
   c. couldn't swim

Breaking Mirrors

Will you have bad luck if you break a mirror? Many people believe this. There is an old story about breaking mirrors.

Long ago, people happened to see their faces in ponds and lakes. Some people were frightened. "That must be my soul," a person would say.

The first mirrors were made of shiny metal. Later, people used glass mirrors. They were careful not to break them. Breaking a mirror could harm the soul. That is how a broken mirror came to mean bad luck. The bad luck is supposed to last for seven years.

You may not believe this story. You may have no bad luck with mirrors. But you should handle mirrors carefully. Pieces from a broken mirror could cut you. They are very sharp.

Choose the best answer for each question.

1. Long ago, people saw their faces in __.
   a. ponds
   b. hands
   c. boats

2. The first mirrors were made of __.
   a. water
   b. shiny metal
   c. glass

3. A face in the mirror was supposed to be the __.
   a. soul
   b. luck
   c. story

4. Breaking a mirror is supposed to bring __ years of bad luck.
   a. five
   b. seven
   c. ten

5. You should handle mirrors __.
   a. with luck
   b. with soul
   c. with care

How To Wash a Car

What is the best way to wash a car? Read these directions to find out.

Use two pails of water and three old towels. Put soap and water in one pail and clean water in the other. Start with the roof of the car and work down. Work on only one part of the car at a time.

Use the soapy water and the first towel to wash the car. Use the clean water and the second towel to rinse. Use the third towel to dry. You will end up with a clean, dry car.

Always wash a car in the shade or early in the evening. Sun causes streaks. You can wax the car after you wash it. Then spray it with cold water and dry it.

Try this tip. Clean white sidewall tires with steel wool soap pads. Rub the tires hard.

Choose the best answer for each question.

1. The directions say to use ___ towels to wash a car.
   a. two
   b. three
   c. many

2. The third towel is for ___ the car.
   a. washing
   b. rinsing
   c. drying

3. What do you do after you wash the car?
   a. You rinse it.
   b. You fix it.
   c. You drive it.

4. Where is the best place to wash a car?
   a. in the sun
   b. in the shade
   c. on the roof

5. Steel wool soap pads are good for cleaning ___.
   a. the tires
   b. the roof
   c. the towels

Golf Without Golf Clubs

People who play golf use golf clubs. Could you play golf without golf clubs? One of the best golfers in the world did. He used a soda-pop bottle instead of golf clubs. He did this trick to make money.

The golfer was Lee Trevino. Lee Trevino is one of the most famous Mexican-American sports stars of all time. He has won more than one million dollars playing golf.

Lee Trevino was not always rich. When he was a young man, he lived in Dallas, Texas. He was very poor. He began working at a small golf course in Dallas. Lee learned a trick to make money. He learned how to hit a golf ball a long way by using a soda-pop bottle. He would hit the ball with the side of the bottle. He knew how to make the ball go just where he wanted it to go. Then he would use the bottom of the bottle to push the ball into the golf hole.

Many people did not believe Lee could do this trick. They wanted to play against him. They would use golf clubs. Lee would use the bottle.

"Many people thought I was a nut," Lee said. "They did not think I could beat them. We would finally agree to play for money."

Lee usually won. He didn't make a lot of money. He did earn a little spending money. Even a little money was important to him.

In 1985, Lee Trevino earned $260,000 playing golf. But by the end of that year, he decided to retire. However, in 1986, he made a comeback and participated in the U.S. Open.

Choose the best answer for each question.

1. People who play golf use ___.
   a. pens
   b. bats
   c. golf clubs

2. Where did Lee Trevino live when he was a young man?
   a. in Dallas
   b. in Mexico
   c. on a golf course

3. Lee Trevino hit a golf ball with ___.
   a. a stick
   b. a soda-pop bottle
   c. a carrot

4. Lee learned his trick ___.
  a. to make money
  b. to stop working
  c. to buy soda pop

5. Lee Trevino earned ___ .
  a. a lot of gold clubs
  b. plenty of money
  c. plenty of bottles

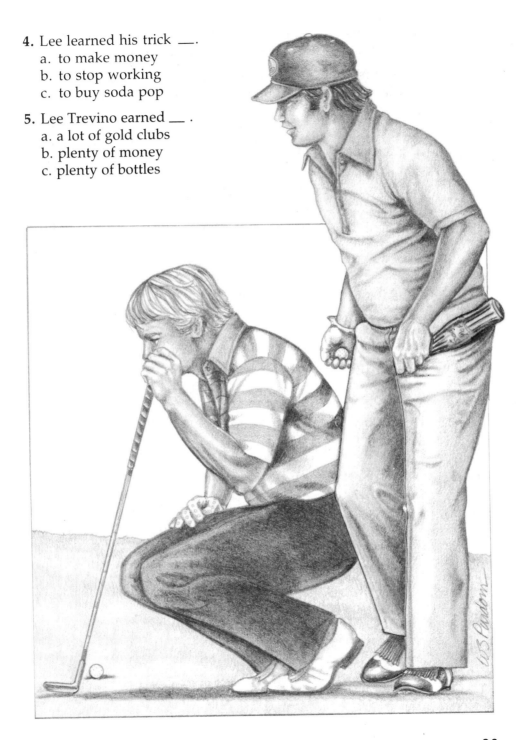

Practice finding details in a reading passage. Follow the test tips on the next four pages. Put your answers on your answer sheet.

Test Tips: In most reading tests, each question has four answers below it. Read all the answers to a question before you choose the best one.

How strong is a dollar bill? A dollar bill lasts about a year and a half. By that time, it is usually worn out. A $5 bill lasts longer. It is not used as often as a dollar bill. A $100 bill lasts longer still.

All the bills are made from the same kind of paper. The paper is very strong. You can fold a bill about 4,000 times before it tears.

Suppose you have a torn bill. You can trade it in at a bank for a whole bill. You must have more than half of the torn bill.

The paper used to print money is different from any other paper. This paper has a special pattern. No one can make the same kind of paper. Besides, making the same kind of paper is against the law.

1. A dollar bill lasts about ___.
   a. one year
   b. a year and a half
   c. two years
   d. ten years

2. Which of the following is true?
   a. A $5 bill lasts longer than a dollar bill.
   b. You can't fold a dollar bill.
   c. You can't tear a dollar bill.
   d. A $100 bill does not last long.

3. The paper used to make bills is ___.
   a. torn
   b. yellow
   c. strong
   d. old

4. How many times can you fold a bill before it tears?
   a. 100 times
   b. 400 times
   c. about 1,000 times
   d. about 4,000 times

5. You can trade in a torn bill if you have ___.
   a. part of a bill
   b. more than half of a bill
   c. two bills
   d. $10

Notice the order of steps in a passage that gives directions. Look back at the steps to answer the questions.

How can you fill a balloon with air without blowing it up? Read these steps.

1. Get a balloon, an empty soda-pop bottle, some baking soda, and some vinegar.
2. Put two teaspoons of baking soda into a balloon.
3. Pour one inch of vinegar into the empty bottle.
4. Put the neck of the balloon tightly over the neck of the bottle.
5. Shake the bottle so that the baking soda will fall in.
6. In a few minutes, the balloon will begin to fill with air.
7. The baking soda and the vinegar mix together to form a gas. This gas fills the balloon.

1. Which step has a list of four things to use?
   a. step 1
   b. step 2
   c. step 4
   d. step 7

2. Where do you put the baking soda?
   a. into an empty bottle
   b. into a balloon
   c. in the air
   d. in a corner

3. How much vinegar should you use?
   a. one spoon
   b. one cup
   c. one inch
   d. one pound

4. When do you shake the bottle?
   a. after step 4
   b. before step 3
   c. before you start
   d. in step 7

5. The baking soda and vinegar mix together to make __.
   a. a balloon
   b. money
   c. a gas
   d. a bottle

Test Tips: Notice dates and other numbers in a reading passage. Be prepared to answer questions about them.

There were no speed limits when the first roads were built in the U.S. Then the number of cars grew. It was safer to have all the cars riding at about the same speed. That is why speed limits were made.

Before 1973, the speed limit on most big roads was 65 miles an hour. Suddenly, the gas supply began to drop. Saving gas became important. One answer was to make a new speed limit of 55 miles an hour.

Fast speeds use up a lot of gas. The new speed limit has saved about three million gallons of gas a day. It has also saved a lot of lives. About 9,000 lives are saved each year. The lower speed gives cars more time to stop.

Some drivers don't pay attention to the speed limit. Drivers in western states think they should be allowed to drive faster. Their roads are flat and straight. Many truck drivers don't like the new speed limit either. They say their trucks run better at 65 miles an hour.

1. The first roads had no __.
   a. cars
   b. signs
   c. lights
   d. speed limits

2. Before 1973, the speed limit was __.
   a. 20 miles an hour
   b. 55 miles an hour
   c. 65 miles an hour
   d. 80 miles an hour

3. A new speed limit of 55 miles an hour was supposed to __.
   a. save gas
   b. build roads
   c. save time
   d. make more cars

4. How many lives have been saved each year since 1973?
   a. 150
   b. about 1,000
   c. about 9,000
   d. about three million

5. Roads in western states are __.
   a. too wide
   b. flat and straight
   c. rocky
   d. made of dirt

On a test, answer the questions you are sure of first. Then go back to the others. Make a mark beside the ones you skipped.

Americans eat more ice cream than anyone else. About 800 million gallons of ice cream are made in just one year in the U.S. That's enough ice cream to make ten ice-cream cones for every person on earth.

Ice cream was not invented in America, though. Rich people in Rome ate ice with honey on top about 2,000 years ago. That was the first ice cream. Milk was added to ice cream hundreds of years later.

In the 1700's, ice cream came to America. George Washington loved ice cream. One summer, our first president spent $200 on his favorite dessert. In those days, ice cream cost a lot of money. By the 1800's, the price went down. Everyone was eating ice cream. Some people tried new ways of making it. A man from Philadelphia made the first ice-cream soda in 1874. After that came the first ice-cream cone and the first chocolate-covered ice cream on a stick.

More vanilla ice cream is sold than any other kind. Chocolate comes in second.

---

1. Rich people ate the first ice cream in ___.
   a. America
   b. Rome
   c. Philadelphia
   d. the U.S.

2. More people ate ice cream in the 1800's because ___.
   a. honey was used
   b. milk was added
   c. the price went down
   d. the price went up

3. Who made the first ice-cream soda?
   a. a man from Philadelphia
   b. a young woman
   c. George Washington
   d. rich people

4. Which of these came last?
   a. ice cream made with milk
   b. the ice-cream soda
   c. ice cream on a stick
   d. ice made with honey

5. Which of the following is true?
   a. The English eat more ice cream than Americans.
   b. George Washington never ate ice cream.
   c. Ice cream came to America in 1874.
   d. More vanilla ice cream is sold than chocolate.

Study the picture on page 28. What is the picture about? What is the main idea? This picture has many details. To find the main idea, add up the details. Then you will know what the picture is about. The questions below will help you find the main idea.

Choose the best answer for each question.

1. The riders in the picture are wearing ___.
   a. shirts and jeans
   b. caps and jackets
   c. shorts and helmets

Check your answer. Look at the riders' clothes. Choose the right details. The answer is **c**.

2. The tires of the bicycles are ___.
   a. thick
   b. thin
   c. blue

Check your answer. What do the tires look like? Find the right detail by checking the picture. The answer is **b**.

3. The bicycles in the picture are ___.
   a. leaning to the side
   b. straight up and down
   c. upside down

Check your answer. You can tell that the bicycles are not straight. They are not upside down, either. The right answer is **a**.

4. Who else is in the picture besides the riders?
   a. a girl who is running
   b. a man who is watching
   c. a woman who is riding

Check your answer. Choose the detail that names the right person. The answer is **b**.

5. What is this picture all about?
   a. a bicycle accident
   b. a bicycle shop
   c. a bicycle race

Check your answer. Add up all the details to find the main idea. The right answer is **c**.

LESSON 1

What is this story about? Add up the details to find the main idea.
Finding the main idea will help you understand the story.

Noise All Around

Noise can harm our hearing. Usually, we hear the best when we are
12 or 13 years old. As we get older, we don't hear as well. How much of
our hearing do we lose? It may depend on the noise around us.

People lose some of their hearing if they work for a long time in noisy
factories. Loud noise goes with other kinds of work, too. A group of
people in New York City had their hearing tested. All of them had lost
some of their hearing. They all had the same kind of job. They were
disc jockeys in dance clubs.

Machines have tested different kinds of noise. A supersonic airplane
makes the loudest noise of all. Sirens, subways, and motorcycles are
other big noise-makers.

Choose the best answer for each question.

1. What is the main idea of this story?
   a. Noise can harm our hearing.
   b. Airplanes are loud.
   c. Cities have too much noise.

Check your answer. The first sentence in this story gives the main idea. It tells what the whole story is about. The words *noise* and *hearing* are in many places in the story. The answer is **a**.

2. Another title for this story could be ___.
   a. "Disc Jockeys"
   b. "Getting Older"
   c. "Noise and Hearing"

Check your answer. A good title tells something about the main idea. Answers **a** and **b** are details in the story, not the main idea. The right answer is **c**.

3. We hear the best when we are ___.
   a. just born
   b. 12 or 13 years old
   c. in factories

Check your answer. The question asks about a detail in the story. Look back at the story to find the right detail. The answer is **b**.

4. ___ in New York City had their hearing tested.
   a. Dancers
   b. Machines
   c. Disc jockeys

Check your answer. Look for words in the story that are like the words in the question. Then find the words that match one of the answers. The answer is **c**.

5. The loudest noise of all comes from ___.
   a. a subway
   b. a factory
   c. a supersonic airplane

Check your answer. Find a sentence like this one near the end of the story. Choose the right words to finish the sentence. The answer is **c**.

The title of this story helps to tell the main idea. Think about the title while you read the story.

Birds Save Lives

Bad weather can come up suddenly at sea. Winds and waves can smash boats. People may end up in the water. When that happens, there is no time to waste. Pigeons may be sent to the rescue.

The pigeons are a special group of birds. The Navy is training these birds to look for the color orange in the water. That is because life jackets are orange.

The pigeons ride in a helicopter with the Navy crew. The birds can see a very long distance — about 2,000 feet. They usually spot the orange life jackets before the crew does. That means the crew can act more quickly to save people.

Anything orange in the water gets the attention of the pigeons. The birds also find orange surfboards that have been lost.

Choose the best answer for each question.

1. The main idea of this story is ___.
   a. how to put on a life jacket
   b. how birds help to save people
   c. how to swim

2. Another title that tells the main idea is ___.
   a. "Pigeons to the Rescue"
   b. "What to Feed Birds"
   c. "Flying Over the Water"

3. A picture of the main idea of this story would show ___.
   a. a bird in the air
   b. birds looking down from a helicopter
   c. children on a boat

4. The pigeons look for the color ___.
   a. blue
   b. red
   c. orange

5. The pigeons also find lost ___.
   a. surfboards
   b. birds
   c. helicopters

Check your answers.

Question 1: In this story, the main idea is not in the first sentence. You must read on to see what the whole story is about. The answer is **b.**

Question 2: A good title tells what the story is mostly about. The answer is **a.**

Question 3: Only one answer tells about the main idea of the story. The answer is **b.**

Question 4: This question asks about a detail. Notice the word *color* in the question. Find the word *color* in the story, and see what color is named. The answer is **c.**

Question 5: Find a sentence like this one at the end of the story. Look for the missing word. The answer is **a.**

Find out what this ad is all about. Look for the main idea while you read the details.

THE MUSIC STORE'S
Great SUMMER SALE!

Save on every record and tape in the store.
POP · ROCK · JAZZ · DISCO · COUNTRY ·

Special low prices on all records and tapes.

LIST PRICE	SALE PRICE
$6.99	$5.99
$7.99	$6.99
$8.99	$7.99

Sale starts June 15 and ends June 29.
No mail or telephone orders during the sale.

THE MUSIC STORE

**38 Park Street
Open Monday–Saturday, 10 a.m. to 6 p.m.**

Choose the best answer for each question.

1. The Music Store is ___.
   a. ordering records
   b. having a sale
   c. closing

2. Which records and tapes in the store are on sale?
   a. all of them
   b. only rock
   c. only jazz and country

3. Records and tapes that cost $7.99 are on sale for ___ .
   a. $5.99
   b. $6.99
   c. $7.99

4. The last day of the sale is ___.
   a. June 15
   b. June 29
   c. Sunday

5. You can't buy records ___.
   a. at 5 o'clock
   b. for low prices
   c. over the phone

Practice finding the main idea and the details in the next stories.

Teaching at Thirteen

Samantha Smith of Manchester, Maine watched a lot of T.V. She listened to news programs regularly and she heard a lot about nuclear war. So she wrote a letter to the head of the Russian government. She asked Yuri Andropov what the Russians were doing to create world peace.

Mr. Andropov wrote back. He invited Samantha and her family to visit him in Russia. There they talked about how their countries could live together peacefully on earth.

Later, Johnny Carson invited her to talk about her trip on *The Tonight Show.* She was seen and heard on T.V. programs around the world. She also wrote a book called *Journey to the Soviet Union.*

Everyone loved this young American girl who liked eating Fruit Roll-Ups and having a sleepover with girlfriends. In 1985 the Russians named a diamond of rare beauty after her.

Although she died in a plane crash when she was only 13, her life was not wasted. She taught people that peace is everybody's business.

Choose the best answer for each question.
1. This story is mainly about ___ .
   a. the Russians
   b. nuclear war
   c. an American girl

2. Another title for this story could be ___ .
   a. "A Young Life"
   b. "A Messenger of Peace"
   c. "Travel in Russia"

3. Samantha contacted Yuri Andropov ___ .
   a. by letter
   b. by messenger
   c. by phone

4. Samantha was invited to ___ .
   a. visit Russia
   b. appear on television
   c. write a book

5. Samantha's life proves that __ .
   a. most kids are useless.
   b. adults can't learn from kids.
   c. anybody can work for world peace.

LESSON 5

Around the World by Bicycle

In 1884, Thomas Stevens decided to ride around the world. He would go by bicycle. No one had done that before. No one has done it the same way since. But first Tom had to learn how to ride a bicycle.

Tom learned quickly. In April, he left his home in San Francisco. He covered 3,000 miles of rough roads. He got to Boston in August. By then, Tom had run out of money. He met the famous Colonel Pope. Pope was a rich man who made and sold bicycles. He agreed to pay for Tom's trip to Europe, so Tom put his bicycle on a boat.

Tom's bike had a giant wheel in front. Sometimes the wheel broke. In Europe, there was always someone to fix it. Tom liked Europe. The roads were good there. There were wonderful things to see. Back home, people read about Tom's trip in the newspapers.

In Asia, the ride got harder. Most people did not speak English. Sometimes people stopped him to look at his bicycle. Animals blocked his path, but Tom rode on. Chinese people gave him gifts. Tom was pleased with the gifts, but they were heavy. The gifts slowed him down. He didn't worry about lost time, though. He was in no hurry.

In January, 1887, Tom returned to San Francisco. He had been away for almost three years. He wrote about his trip and gave talks. He became well known. He made enough money to live on. Tom's long ride really paid off!

Choose the best answer for each question.

1. This story is mostly about ___.
   a. animals in Asia
   b. a man who saw the world on a bicycle
   c. a new kind of bicycle

2. Colonel Pope paid for ___.
   a. Tom's trip to Europe
   b. a new bicycle
   c. a hamburger dinner

3. Tom liked Europe because ___.
   a. he made money
   b. the roads were good
   c. his wheel broke

4. At home, people found out about Tom's trip ___.
   a. on the radio
   b. from Chinese people
   c. from newspapers

5. Tom rode slowly in Asia because ___.
   a. his gifts were heavy
   b. he did not speak English
   c. his bicycle broke

The Road That Fell In

A young man and his date were driving home from a party one winter night in 1973. They lived in Swansea, a city in Great Britain. The young people talked quietly on their way home.

Suddenly, all talk stopped. Something had happened. The road in front of their car had disappeared!

The front end of the car tipped forward. The driver hit the brakes. The car slid for a few seconds. Then the back wheels caught on a patch of road. The car came to a stop. In front, there was no more road. There was only a deep, black pit.

At first, the two young people sat frozen. Any move might send the car over the edge. Slowly, they made their way to the doors. They jumped onto safe ground and looked down. The front of the car was hanging over a big, wide hole. The hole seemed to have no bottom.

The police came and pulled the car back. The young people were safe. What had happened? A few days later, they found out. The road didn't just disappear. It fell into an old coal mine. Many roads in Swansea are built over old coal mines. Heavy weights, like cars, can make the roads fall in.

Choose the best answer for each question.

1. This story is mostly about ___.
   a. a party in Swansea
   b. driving in the winter
   c. a road that disappeared

2. A picture of the main idea of this story would show ___.
   a. a car in a hole
   b. a car at the edge of a pit
   c. a policeman in a car

3. The young people in the story lived in ___.
   a. Swansea
   b. a coal mine
   c. France

4. The back wheels caught on the road and ___.
   a. stopped the car
   b. pushed the car
   c. fell off

5. Many roads in Swansea are built on top of ___.
   a. water
   b. heavy weights
   c. coal mines

The Tree of Life

Two travelers are walking in Africa. The sun beats down on them. The land is dry and dusty. Even the rivers have dried up.

The travelers sit down next to a huge, ugly tree. They're hot and tired. Most of all, they're thirsty. They reach for their water canteen. It's empty! Where can they find water? They look up at the tree next to them. Then they remember. Quickly, they climb to the top of the tree. They find a scooped-out hole there. The hole is filled with water. The travelers take huge gulps. The baobab tree has saved their lives.

The baobab tree is a funny-looking tree. Its bark is wrinkled and looks like elephant skin. The branches look like roots reaching for the sky. But this strange tree has saved the lives of people and animals. The tree stores enough water at the top to last for many months. Animals use the tree as a drinking fountain. Some animals even move in and live among the roots. The animals can stay for a long time. Some baobab trees live for 2,000 years.

Choose the best answer for each question.

1. This story is mainly about ___.
   a. animals in trees
   b. the hot sun in Africa
   c. a tree with water in it

2. Another title that tells the main idea is ___.
   a. "Climbing a Tree"
   b. "The Baobab Tree"
   c. "Elephant Skin"

3. The travelers in this story are ___.
   a. thirsty
   b. laughing
   c. children

4. The water in a baobab tree is ___.
   a. in the roots
   b. full of salt
   c. at the top

5. Animals that live in the tree ___.
   a. are not in Africa
   b. can stay for many years
   c. can't get water

LESSON 8

Pleasant Dreams

Dreams may be more important than sleep. Some people don't need very much sleep. But we all need to dream, scientists say.

Dreams take up about one quarter of our sleeping time. People have several dreams each night. Dreams are like short movies. They are usually in color. Some dreams are like *old* movies. They come to us over and over again. That may be because the dreamer is worrying about something. Dreaming may be a way of trying to find an answer.

Some people get new ideas about their work from dreams. They could have been thinking about their work all day. These thoughts can carry over into dreams.

Sometimes we wake up with a good feeling from a dream. But often we can't remember the dream. Dreams can disappear quickly from memory.

Too much dreaming can be harmful. The more we sleep, the longer we dream. The mind is hard at work when we dream. That is why we may have a long sleep and still wake up tired.

44

Choose the best answer for each question.

1. The main idea of the story is that __.
   a. people need to dream
   b. people like to sleep
   c. dreams are like movies

2. Another title for the story could be __.
   a. "Secret Dreams"
   b. "The Longest Sleep"
   c. "All About Dreams"

3. It may be more important to dream than to __.
   a. think
   b. sleep
   c. work

4. Dreams and movies are usually __.
   a. very long
   b. in color
   c. about work

5. Which of these ideas is in the story?
   a. We always remember dreams.
   b. All dreams are happy.
   c. Long dreams can make you tired.

TAKING TESTS

Practice finding the main idea in a reading selection. Follow the test tips on the next four pages. Put your answers on your answer sheet.

Test Tips: The title of a story helps to tell the main idea. Sometimes a story on a test has no title. Then you can usually find the main idea in the first few sentences.

Fires kill thousands of people every year. Learn what to do in case a fire breaks out. Here are some rules to follow at home.

The first thing to do is to make an escape plan. In a fire, smoke and flames may block stairs or a hallway. Plan a way to get out of each room in your home. You may have to climb out through a window. At night, sleep with the door closed.

Don't try to fight a fire yourself. Get away from the fire and call the fire department. Test a door with your hands before you open it. Don't open a door that is warm. Use another way out.

Many fires start in a kitchen. A pan of grease may catch fire. Put a lid on the pan and turn off the stove. Never use water on a grease fire because water will spread the fire.

1. What is the best title for this selection?
   a. "Racing to a Fire"
   b. "Lives Lost in Fires"
   c. "What To Do in Case of Fire"
   d. "Safe Cooking"

2. An escape plan is __.
   a. a way to fight a fire
   b. a way to get out
   c. a way to sleep
   d. a way to cook

3. Do not open a door that is __.
   a. warm
   b. greasy
   c. wet
   d. closed

4. One rule in the story is to __.
   a. pull the fire alarm
   b. sleep with the door closed
   c. climb on the roof
   d. put out the fire yourself

5. Which one of these ideas is in the story?
   a. All fires start in a kitchen.
   b. Windows keep out smoke.
   c. Wood burns quickly.
   d. Water will spread a grease fire.

Small children like to eat snow. Sometimes they make snow cones.
But eating snow can be dangerous. The snow may be full of lead.

The air in cities has a lot of lead in it. Country air may have less. Most
of the lead comes from cars. Snow falls and it soaks up the lead from
the air. More lead is trapped in the snow on the ground.

Even a little lead in the body can be dangerous. Lead can harm the
brain. The body gets rid of lead very slowly, so bits of lead can build
up.

Children often lick icicles hanging from a roof. That is even more
dangerous than eating snow. The water in icicles runs off the roof and
picks up lead. The lead builds up as the icicles grow longer.

1. What is the main idea of this
   story?
   a. Eating snow is dangerous.
   b. Cities have a lot of snow.
   c. Country air is clean.
   d. Lead comes from cars.

2. Which of these is the best title
   for this selection?
   a. "How Water Turns to Ice"
   b. "Cleaning City Streets"
   c. "Please Don't Eat the Snow"
   d. "Snow Cones"

3. The story says that snow may
   be full of __.
   a. icicles
   b. air
   c. cones
   d. lead

4. Most of the lead in the air
   comes from __.
   a. snow
   b. cars
   c. children
   d. bottles

5. Children should not lick icicles
   because __.
   a. icicles are cold
   b. snow cones are better
   c. icicles can be full of lead
   d. a roof is dangerous

Test Tips: Sometimes each paragraph in a story has a different main idea. Notice where each paragraph begins.

In the fall, the oval leaves of the Colorado aspen trees turn bright gold. Their long leaf stalks cause the leaves to tremble in the slightest breeze. Many people travel from all over the country to see this shimmering foliage display.

Some people, however, see more than the golden color of the aspen leaves. They see gold. Treenappers uproot the trees and sell them for $10 and $15 to nurseries and landscapers. An average treenapper can even make as much as $45 an hour by selling the trees from door to door. There is a great demand for these beautiful trees.

By day, the thieves enter the forest with other tourists. They dig up hundreds of saplings. They ball the roots in burlap and ease them back into their holes. Later, when the area is patrolled, the forest rangers cannot tell that the young trees have been dug up. Then the treenappers return at night. They load their booty into trucks and disappear into the darkness.

If caught, these thieves face a sentence of 10 years in jail. They can also be fined $10,000 for stealing government property. The forest rangers have found many holes, but have yet to catch their first aspen thief.

Choose the best answer to each question.

1. The first paragraph in the selection is mainly about __ .
   a. Colorado
   b. aspen trees
   c. forest rangers
   d. treenapping

2. What is true about the aspen tree?
   a. The natural color of its leaves is gold.
   b. The color of its leaves turns gold in the fall.
   c. People find gold in its roots.
   d. It can grow in a burlap sack.

3. Which of these is the best title for this selection?
   a. Colorado in the Fall
   b. The Treenappers
   c. To Catch the Aspen Thief
   d. Thieves For Gold

4. Forest rangers have caught __ treenappers.
   a. many
   b. few
   c. some
   d. no

5. Trees in a national forest belong to the __ .
   a. government
   b. forest rangers
   c. tourists
   d. treenappers

Test Tips: A poem has a main idea, like a story. Read a poem quickly the first time. You'll find the main idea more easily.

Wake
gently this morning
to a different day.
Listen.
There is no bray
of buses,
no brake growls,
no siren howls and
no horns
blow.
There is only
the silence
of a city
hushed
by snow.

Lilian Moore

1. What is the main idea of the poem?
   a. Waking up is hard.
   b. Cities are noisy places.
   c. Snow has made the city quiet.
   d. Nights are quiet times.

2. What is the best title for the poem?
   a. "Waking Up Late"
   b. "A Snowy Morning"
   c. "A Winter Day"
   d. "Bus Travel"

3. What has snow brought to the city?
   a. silence   c. buses
   b. horns   d. snowballs

4. Why does the poet say this day is "different"?
   a. There is no snow.
   b. There are no trees.
   c. There are no horns or sirens.
   d. There are no people.

5. A picture of the main idea of this poem would show ___.
   a. a traffic jam
   b. trees and flowers
   c. an alarm clock
   d. a snow-covered city street

PART 3

Inference

You probably don't know the woman in the picture on page 50. But you can figure out what she is like. Use the details in the picture to help you. The following questions ask about these details.

Choose the best answer for each question.

1. The woman must know that the ducks like to ___.
   a. swim away
   b. come to get food
   c. climb the rocks

Check your answer. Look back at the details in the picture. The woman is standing and waiting with some food. The answer is **b**.

2. What is the weather in the picture?
   a. It is sunny.
   b. It is raining.
   c. It is snowing.

Check your answer. Did you notice the umbrella? There is no snow in the picture. So the answer must be **b**.

3. The cloth bag is for ___.
   a. carrying the food
   b. holding the umbrella
   c. catching a duck

Check your answer. The food in the woman's hand must have come from the bag. The answer is **a**.

4. The woman must think that feeding ducks is ___.
   a. silly
   b. important
   c. boring

Check your answer. The woman is willing to come out in the rain and stand on slippery rocks. The answer is **b**.

5. What probably happened right after this picture was taken?
   a. The ducks swam away.
   b. The woman went home.
   c. A duck grabbed the food.

Check your answer. Study the picture and think about the next part of the action. The answer is **c**.

LESSON 1

The answer to a question is not always in the story. You can tell what seems to be true, however. You can use the details in the story to figure out an answer. Read the next story.

The Eyes in the Window

One night, a burglar alarm went off at a store in England. The store sold clothes for men. A policeman came to search the store. He didn't find anything, so he got ready to leave.

Outside, he looked back at the store's large window. The figures wearing new clothes were lined up in the window. They looked real, but they weren't real. Or were they?

The policeman turned on his flashlight. He looked at the faces in the window. One pair of eyes blinked at him. Then the policeman knew the answer. He had found the burglar.

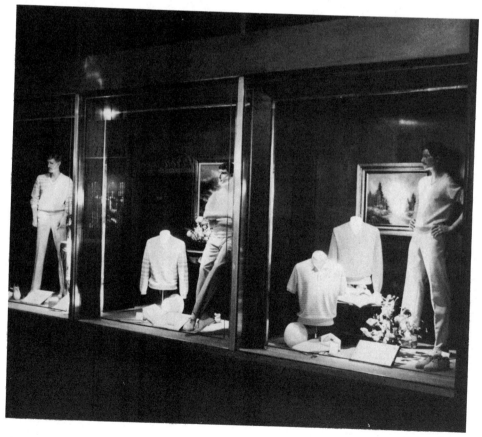

Choose the best answer for each question.

1. The burglar was __.
    a. on the roof
    b. outside in a car
    c. in the store window

Check your answer. The answer is not in the story. The details can help you guess the answer. The right answer is **c**.

2. The policeman knew that only a real person could __.
    a. blink his eyes
    b. stand in the dark
    c. be in a window

Check your answer. Look back at the last few sentences of the story. The words in these sentences can help you find the answer. The right answer is **a**.

3. The burglar must have been __.
    a. jumping around
    b. standing very still
    c. wearing old clothes

Check your answer. From reading the story, you know that the burglar was trying to hide. Choose the answer that makes sense. The answer is **b**.

4. What must have caused the eyes to blink?
    a. the burglar alarm
    b. the light from the flashlight
    c. the clothes in the window

Check your answer. Use the details in the last paragraph to figure out the right answer. The answer is **b**.

5. What is the main idea of this story?
    a. buying clothes
    b. a policeman's day
    c. catching a burglar

Check your answer. What is the story about? Add up the details in the story to find the main idea. The right answer is **c**.

Think about the facts in this story. Then decide what seems to be true about robots.

The Robots Are Coming

Robots are becoming a big part of our lives. There may be half a million robots in the U.S. 20 years from now.

These machines are changing the way work is being done. Thousands of robots are used in factories. These robots are not like the robots in movies. They don't walk or talk. Instead, a robot may be just a metal arm. The robot arm can do a certain job in a factory over and over again. It can do jobs that people may not want to do. A robot never gets tired of doing the same thing.

Sometimes a robot gets to do more exciting work. In Canada, police are using a robot on wheels. This robot's job is to take apart bombs that may go off.

Choose the best answer for each question.

1. Robots are getting ___.
   a. more important
   b. less important
   c. more like people

2. Robots are probably put in factories to ___.
   a. talk to the people
   b. be in the movies
   c. get the work done faster

3. Another title for this story could be ___.
   a. "Robots in Our Lives"
   b. "A Job in a Factory"
   c. "Robot on Wheels"

4. A robot in a factory would not ___.
   a. need new parts
   b. move back and forth
   c. fall asleep

5. The robot in Canada can probably ___.
   a. build a bomb
   b. save lives
   c. work on a farm

Check your answers.

Question 1: The first two sentences in the story can help you figure out the right answer. The answer is **a.**

Question 2: Notice the word *probably* in the question. You will have to figure out what is true. Use the facts in the second paragraph. The answer is **c.**

Question 3: A good title tells the main idea of the story. Answers **b** and **c** are details in the story. The right answer is **a.**

Question 4: The story says that a robot never gets tired. Use that fact when you choose an answer. The answer is **c.**

Question 5: Find the word *Canada* in the last part of the story. Read the facts in that paragraph. Choose the answer that seems to be true. The answer is **b.**

Read the next selections and figure out what seems to be true.

Are You an Owl or a Lark?

Do you start the day very slowly, and really wake up in the afternoon? Then you may be an *owl*. Are you full of pep in the morning and tired out later on? Then you may be a *lark*.

Owls and larks are different kinds of birds. Scientists use these names for different kinds of people, too. *Owls* are people who take more time to wake up. They seem to have more pep as the day goes on. *Larks* are people who are wide awake and busy right away. They may slow down in the afternoon.

The way we feel affects the kind of work we do. Larks do better work in the morning. They are more wide awake then. Owls do better work in the afternoon or at night. That can make a difference in a job or at school. Larks would probably do better on school tests first thing in the morning. Owls would do better later in the day.

Decide how *you* feel at different hours of the day. Try to save your hardest work for your best hours.

Choose the best answer for each question.

1. People who are called *larks* __.
   a. are wide awake early
   b. sleep all morning
   c. like to play music

2. An *owl* must be a bird that __.
   a. gets up early
   b. eats all day
   c. stays awake late

3. You could be called a *lark* if you __.
   a. sleep until noon
   b. jump out of bed early
   c. sit in a tree

4. A person called an *owl* would want to __.
   a. take a test late in the day
   b. take a test in the morning
   c. learn how to fly

5. What is the main idea of this story?

    a. Owls and larks are birds.

    b. People are as different as larks and owls.

    c. Owls are good pets.

Sea Mail

Some people don't need a mailbox to send a message. They use a bottle instead. Here are two stories about people who sent a message in a bottle. Both stories are true.

In 1956, a sailor from Sweden was on a ship. He wrote a letter, asking any young woman to write to him. He put the letter in a bottle and threw the bottle into the sea.

Two years later, a man found the bottle on a beach in Italy. He read the letter and showed it to his daughter. She was 18. As a joke, she wrote to the sailor. They began to exchange letters. In a few months, they were married.

Here is the second story. Back in 1924, a boy from Arkansas wrote his name on the back of his picture. He put the picture in a bottle and dropped the bottle into a river.

The bottle was not found for many years. Then one day a man named Bill picked it up on a beach in Florida. He pulled the picture out of the bottle and looked at it. He could hardly believe his eyes. The boy in the picture was his old friend, Tom, from Arkansas. Bill had not seen Tom for 25 years. Somehow the bottle had come to the right place.

Choose the best answer for each question.

1. What is the main idea of the whole story?
   a. sailing on a ship
   b. sending a message in a bottle
   c. sending a message to Italy

2. After the sailor wrote a letter, he ___.
   a. threw the letter away
   b. put the letter in a bottle
   c. found a bottle on a beach

3. The sailor and the girl from Italy ___.
   a. grew up together
   b. went to the same school
   c. had not known each other

4. The man named Bill looked at the picture of Tom and was ___.
   a. unhappy
   b. surprised
   c. tired

5. At the end of the story, Bill and Tom must have been ___.
   a. 12 years old
   b. 25 years old
   c. more than 25 years old

INFERENCE LESSON 5

Do the Animals Know?

Many animals do strange things before an earthquake. This news may be important. Earthquakes can kill people and knock down homes. The animals may help to save lives.

Some animals make a lot of noise before an earthquake. Farmers have told about this. Dogs that are usually quiet have started to howl. Horses on farms have run around in circles. Mice have left their holes and run away. Cows have given less milk.

In a town in Italy, cats raced down the street in a group. That happened only a few hours before an earthquake. In San Francisco, a man kept tiny pet frogs. One Sunday, the frogs jumped around more than ever. They made loud noises, like bigger frogs. That night, an earthquake struck the city.

People want to know when an earthquake is coming. Then they could get away safely. Right now, there is no sure way to know ahead of time. Maybe the best idea is to watch the animals.

Choose the best answer for each question.

1. This story is mostly about ___.
   a. how animals act before an earthquake
   b. how an earthquake starts
   c. how mice leave their homes

2. Before an earthquake, quiet dogs ___.
   a. ran away
   b. started to howl
   c. climbed trees

3. Before an earthquake, the frogs ___.
   a. sang
   b. left their homes
   c. jumped around a lot

4. There have been earthquakes in ___.
   a. most countries
   b. Italy and San Francisco
   c. Chicago and Spain

5. People want to ___.
  a. be in an earthquake
  b. find out early about an earthquake
  c. run around in circles

Fernando

Fernando has a basketball.
He tap, tap, taps it down the hall,
then leaps up high and shoots with care.
The fact a basket isn't there,
he totally dismisses.
He says he never misses.
My crazy friend Fernando.

Marci Ridlon

Choose the best answer for each question.

1. This poem is about ___.
   a. a basketball game
   b. a boy with a basketball
   c. tap dancing

2. In the second line of the poem, Fernando ___ the ball.
   a. bounces
   b. throws
   c. catches

3. Where does Fernando shoot the basketball?
   a. in the gym
   b. in the hall
   c. in a classroom

4. How does Fernando shoot the basketball?
   a. hard
   b. with one hand
   c. carefully

5. Fernando doesn't care that ___.
   a. he has no ball
   b. the ball is flat
   c. there is no basket

The Cat That Showed Up

Li Ping was the pet cat of a young woman named Vivian. Vivian lived in Ohio. She decided to take a job in Florida. She could not take Li Ping with her right away, so she left the cat with her sister.

In a month, Vivian found a good place to live. She wrote to her sister and asked her to send Li Ping to Florida. Vivian missed her cat very much. She mailed the letter and went to visit a friend. She started up the steps of her friend's house. Suddenly, something caught her eye. A cat was coming toward her. It looked thin and very hungry.

"That cat looks like Li Ping," thought Vivian. But it couldn't be. Li Ping was more than a thousand miles away. The cat ran straight to Vivian. She picked it up and looked at it. The cat opened its mouth and let out a tiny squeak. Then Vivian knew the cat was hers. Li Ping got hurt when he was a kitten. The only sound he could make was a little squeak.

Vivian called her sister in Ohio. Li Ping had been missing for two weeks, her sister said. She was afraid to tell Vivian. She knew how much Vivian loved her cat.

How did Li Ping make such a long trip? How did the cat find Vivian? She was not even at her own home. No one knows the answers to those questions. No one knows how a cat's mind works.

Choose the best answer for each question.

1. Vivian moved to Florida so she could __.
   a. start a new job
   b. find a new cat
   c. visit a friend

2. The only sound Li Ping could make was __.
   a. a growl
   b. a squeak
   c. a scream

3. At first Vivian could not tell if the cat was Li Ping because __.
   a. it was running
   b. it looked thin and hungry
   c. it got hurt

4. The story does not tell __.
   a. why Vivian left Ohio
   b. where Vivian moved
   c. how Li Ping got to Florida

5. Another title for this story could be __.
   a. "Cats in Florida"
   b. "The Strange Story of Li Ping"
   c. "How To Care for a Cat"

Living in the Yukon

The Yukon is different from most places. It is a part of Canada. The Yukon is bigger than California. Not many people live in the Yukon. There are some good reasons for that.

The winters in the Yukon are very cold. Sometimes the temperature goes down to 40° F below zero. Cars won't start in such cold air. People have to keep a fire going near the car.

Homes in the Yukon are usually log cabins. There are no electric lights or telephones in most of the Yukon. Water may have to be carried from a creek. A home can be hundreds of miles from the nearest town.

Living in the Yukon is certainly not easy. Some people from the U.S. move there anyway. A man and his wife lived in a big town in New Jersey and moved to the Yukon. They like the open space there. They are getting used to new adventures.

One day the woman noticed some sugar spilled in her kitchen. She thought she heard her husband outside, and she went to ask him about the sugar. She came face to face with a black bear. The bear was growling and coming closer. She shut the door fast. "That doesn't happen much in New Jersey," she said.

Choose the best answer for each question.

1. The Yukon is a part of __.
   a. Canada
   b. California
   c. the water

2. What is the main idea of this story?
   a. warming up a cold car
   b. living in the Yukon
   c. catching a bear

3. Many houses in the Yukon have no __.
   a. kitchens
   b. windows
   c. running water

4. People who live in the Yukon probably don't have __.
   a. cars
   b. warm coats
   c. many neighbors

5. The one who spilled the sugar was probably ___.
   a. the bear
   b. the woman
   c. the husband

The Story of Harriet Quimby

Should a woman fly an airplane? Most people in the early 1900's said no. A woman named Harriet Quimby lived during those years. Harriet loved airplanes. She made up her mind to fly one.

She found someone to teach her, and soon she became a good pilot. In 1912, Harriet made a plan. She would fly from England to France, 22 miles across the water. No woman had ever done that.

Her friends told her not to go. Flying was dangerous in those days. Airplanes were small. They were made of wood and bicycle wheels. Sometimes they fell apart in the air.

Harriet wasn't worried. On April 16, 1912, she was ready to go. She started her plane and took off. She climbed to 1,500 feet and turned toward France. She looked down. Everything was covered with fog! Harriet kept going. She thought she might be over land. She let the plane drop lower. Then the fog cleared. A sandy beach was below her. Harriet landed right on the beach. She was in France. The trip had taken only 30 minutes.

"Any woman could do it," said Harriet.

Choose the best answer for each question.

1. Harriet Quimby showed that she __.
   a. was afraid of flying
   b. didn't give up
   c. wanted to get hurt

2. Another title for this story could be __.
   a. "How To Fly a Plane"
   b. "Around the World in a Plane"
   c. "The Woman Who Wanted To Fly"

3. Anyone could have gone from England to France __.
   a. by car
   b. by boat
   c. by bicycle

4. Long ago, small airplanes were made of __.
   a. wood and bicycle wheels
   b. wood and paper
   c. glass and metal

5. In 1912, planes couldn't land ___.
   a. on their wheels
   b. on a beach
   c. in the fog

Golden Slopes

Bill Johnson feels that if he hadn't learned to do something well, he would be in prison today. He won the U.S. Olympic gold medal for skiing in 1984. But he was not always the good All-American hero.

When he was about 16 years old, he was arrested for stealing a car. He was conditionally released. While under a law officer's supervision in Wenatchee, Washington, he went to school to improve his skiing.

Later he became part of the U.S. Olympic team. But he did not behave well. He was nasty and insulted many people. He wanted all the attention for himself. He refused to listen to his coach. So he was thrown off the team.

He wrote a letter to his coach and apologized for his behavior. He asked for a second chance. His coach felt that Bill had grown up by then. He believed that he would be a good member of the team. Bill was allowed to ski in the 1984 Olympics.

His speed and style made Bill Johnson the hero of the Alpine skiing events. He proved that people are not born heroes. They have to work hard and believe in themselves. Then they become heroes.

Choose the best answer to each question.

1. What did Bill Johnson win the Olympic gold medal for?
   a. skating
   b. running
   c. skiing

2. Bill Johnson was __ .
   a. not always a hero
   b. always a hero
   c. never a hero

3. At first the Olympic ski team __ .
   a. admired Bill Johnson
   b. did not want to ski with him
   c. thought he was their best skier

4. Bill got back on the team because __ .
   a. he realized he had been wrong
   b. he proved he could ski well
   c. the coach liked him

The Desert

This is no place
for anyone
who wants
soft hills
and meadows
and everything
green
green
green....

This is for hawks
that like only
the loneliest canyons
and lizards
that run
in the hottest sand
and
coyotes
that choose
the rockiest trails.

It's for them.

And for
hard skinny plants
that do without water
for months
at a time.

Byrd Baylor

Choose the best answer for each question.

1. The place this poem tells about is ___.
    a. the city
    b. the park
    c. the desert

2. The desert is no place for anyone who likes ___.
    a. hot sand
    b. dry land
    c. swimming in lakes

3. A picture of the main idea of this poem would show ___.
    a. a place with sand and rocks
    b. a place with grass and trees
    c. a place with a river

4. Hard skinny plants grow in a place that is ___.
    a. soft and green
    b. cold and wet
    c. hot and dry

5. What other animals might be happy in the desert?
    a. alligators
    b. snakes
    c. fish

LESSON 12

The Picture-Taking Man

In Harlem, people called James Van Der Zee "the picture-taking man." Harlem is a part of New York City. James came to Harlem from Lenox, a town in Massachusetts. He was the first person in Lenox to own a camera. That was in 1901. James was 14 then. He took pictures of his family and other people in Lenox.

James moved to Harlem in 1908. Many young black people were moving there. He wanted to play music, not take pictures. After six years, he opened his first picture-taking shop. He could make more money selling his pictures than playing music.

Almost everyone in Harlem was in his pictures. He took pictures of families and parades and parties. He took pictures of soldiers before they went to fight in wars. His pictures showed the neighborhoods of Harlem.

Many people didn't know about his work. Then a museum used some of his pictures in a show. The world found out about James Van Der Zee and his pictures.

James spent most of his life taking pictures. In his last years, he took pictures of famous people, such as Bill Cosby and Muhammad Ali. He always thought his pictures could be better. He said, "The camera was never able to get enough." In 1983, at the age of 96, James Van Der Zee died of a heart attack. His pictures will live forever.

Choose the best answer for each question.

1. James Van Der Zee owned the only camera in Lenox __.
   a. when he was 14
   b. when he was 94
   c. in 1908

2. Where did James Van Der Zee spend most of his life?
   a. in Lenox
   b. on a farm
   c. in Harlem

3. Another title for this story could be __.
   a. "The Man Who Played Music"
   b. "The Life of James Van Der Zee"
   c. "How To Take Pictures"

4. James Van Der Zee's pictures mostly showed ___ .
   a. people playing music
   b. flowers in a garden
   c. how people lived in Harlem

5. What did James Van Der Zee think about his pictures?
   a. He thought they were too small.
   b. He thought they were not good enough.
   c. He thought they were funny.

This picture shows James Van Der Zee as a young man in Harlem.

Practice using details to figure out what a story means. Follow the test tips on the next three pages. Put your answers on your answer sheet.

Test Tips: Numbers in a story can help you answer questions. Try to figure out why the numbers are important.

Long ago, the sky over California was full of condors. Today, the sky is full of airplanes. People have taken over the condor's space. These big birds with giant wings are dying out.

Condors once flew along the Pacific Coast from Canada to Mexico. Then people moved into woods where the birds lived. By 1970, there were only about 50 condors left along the coast. Now there are less than 30. None of these birds may be left in 20 years.

Most people think the condors should be saved. People have different ideas for helping the birds. One group of people wants to study the birds and find out where they go. They also want to take the birds to zoos so that baby condors can be born there. A second group of people wants to leave the birds alone. Instead, they want to protect the wild places where the birds live.

1. What must have been true about condors long ago?
   a. There were only a few.
   b. There were 20.
   c. There were 50.
   d. There were many.

2. The number of condors in California is __.
   a. growing
   b. staying the same
   c. getting smaller
   d. about 200

3. Which of these is the best title for this article?
   a. "The Sky Over California"
   b. "Saving the Condors"
   c. "Birds of America"
   d. "Big Birds in Zoos"

4. People want to help the condors but __.
   a. the birds will not let them
   b. they can't agree on how to do it
   c. hunters keep killing the birds
   d. there are too many birds

5. Baby condors in a zoo would __.
   a. get good care
   b. fly away
   c. get smaller
   d. live in a house

Test Tips: Before you look at the four answers, decide on *your* answer. Then see if one of the answers matches yours. There is a good chance that this answer will be the right one.

Banana Eskimo Pops

6 bananas
1 package (6 ounces) semi-sweet chocolate pieces
1 cup chopped peanuts
12 wooden popsicle sticks

Peel the bananas. Cut them in half the long way. Put a wooden stick in an end of each banana half. Put the bananas in a low pan. Freeze them for 2 to 3 hours.

Melt the chocolate pieces slowly in a pot over hot water. Use a knife to spread the melted chocolate over all the bananas. Sprinkle with the nuts quickly, before the chocolate gets hard.

Wrap each pop in foil or plastic wrap. Keep them in the freezer. Serves 12.

1. The foods you need are in a list at the top so you can __.
   a. taste them
   b. have them ready
   c. chop them
   d. freeze them

2. The wooden stick in the banana is for __.
   a. holding the pop
   b. cutting the pop
   c. peeling the banana
   d. freezing the banana

3. The reason you melt the chocolate is to __.
   a. cut it
   b. wrap it
   c. eat it
   d. spread it

4. What will happen if the chocolate gets hard too fast?
   a. The chocolate will melt.
   b. The peanuts will not stick.
   c. The bananas will not freeze.
   d. The hot water won't boil.

5. Six bananas can make 12 pops because __.
   a. the bananas are cut in small pieces
   b. the bananas are large
   c. each pop is made of half a banana
   d. the chocolate makes the bananas bigger

Test Tips: A question after a story may begin with "Why." The answer may not be in the story. Use the facts in the story to choose an answer.

The year was 1849. Americans were moving west across the country. Men set up camps near gold fields. Early settlers built their homes on open land. The Army got busy building forts.

All of these people needed the same kind of help. They needed food, clothes, and other goods. A few brave men came to help. They were the "truckers" of the old West.

The early truckers carried goods, like the truckers of today. But they didn't have trucks then. They used long lines of wagons. Mules or oxen pulled the wagons. The trips were dangerous. The truckers had to fight off robbers. The roads were bad.

One of the early truckers was William Russell. In one year, his company sent out two and a half million pounds of goods from Kansas. His business grew, until 1868. In that year, railroad trains began to steam across the country.

1. Why couldn't people in the old West get their goods fast?
   a. They had no money.
   b. They lived far from towns.
   c. They grew their own food.
   d. The weather was bad.

2. This story is mostly about ___.
   a. truckers of the old West
   b. William Russell
   c. gold fields
   d. new highways

3. The truckers of the old West are like today's ___.
   a. airplane pilots
   b. bus drivers
   c. bicycle riders
   d. long-distance truckers

4. The wagons from Kansas carried ___ .
   a. radios and TV's
   b. clothes and food
   c. zoo animals
   d. gold

5. Why did the wagons lose business after 1868?
   a. There were no roads.
   b. There were no drivers.
   c. Railroads carried the goods.
   d. Airplanes carried the goods.

UNIT II
VOCABULARY

PART 1: *Words and Meaning*   80

PART 2: *Context Clues*   112

PART 3: *Words with Several Meanings*   128

PART 4: *Word Parts*   140

PART 1 *Words and Meaning*

In Part 1, you are going to learn about three different ways to explain the meanings of new words. You will learn to match words that have the same meaning, words that have opposite meanings, and words that sound alike.

Look at the objects in the picture below. Can you find two objects that are used to do almost the same thing? Can you find two objects that are used to do opposite things? Can you find two objects whose names sound alike?

Every word has a meaning. Sometimes two words have almost the same meaning. Knowing about words that have the same meaning can help you read better.

Sometimes you will see a hard word in your reading. Maybe you can think of another word that has almost the same meaning as the hard word. Thinking of the easier word will help you understand the hard word better. It will also help you better understand the ideas you are reading.

Read the short paragraph below. Two of the words are in dark type.

Many laws that were passed years ago seem very **foolish** today. Some of these laws are still listed in law books. Here are two examples. An Alaskan law says that a person cannot **disturb** a grizzly bear by taking its photograph. In Blythe, California, a person must own two cows to be allowed to wear cowboy boots.

One of the words in dark type means almost the same as *bother*. Which word do you think means *bother*?

One of the words in dark type means almost the same as *silly*. Which word do you think means *silly*?

Read the paragraph again. This time read the word *silly* in place of **foolish**. Also read the word *bother* in place of **disturb**. Did using the easier words help you understand the paragraph better?

Do the activities on the next two pages. You will learn more about words that have almost the same meaning.

A. Look at the words in List 1 below. They were all used on page 81. You will find a word or phrase with the same meaning in List 2. Can you match the words that have the same meaning? Put your answers on your paper.

LIST 1
1. foolish
2. laws
3. some
4. photograph
5. wear

LIST 2
a. rules
b. put on
c. silly
d. picture
e. several

Check your answers. Reread the paragraph on page 81. Read the words in List 2 in place of the words in List 1. Does the paragraph still make sense to you? If it does, then your answers are right.

B. Read the next paragraph about more silly laws. Notice the words in dark type.

There are many **unusual** laws about husbands and wives. A strange Cleveland law says people are not **permitted** to get married while they are wearing bathing suits. They must be dressed in other clothes. In Vermont, a woman cannot walk down the street **solo** on Sunday. Her husband must follow 20 **paces** behind her. In Lebanon, Tennessee, a husband is **forbidden** to kick his wife out of bed. He is not allowed to kick her out even if she has cold feet.

Now try to answer these questions. You will find the answers in the paragraph on page 82.

1. Which word means almost the same as *alone?*
2. Which word means almost the same as *strange?*
3. Which word means almost the same as *steps?*
4. Which word means almost the same as *allowed?*
5. Which word means almost the same as *not allowed?*

Check your answers. Reread the paragraph. Put the words from the questions in place of the words in dark type. Does the paragraph still make sense to you? If it does, your answers are right.

C. Here are the kinds of questions you sometimes see on a vocabulary test. Look at the word in dark type at the top of each item. Then pick the answer that means the same as the word in dark type. Put your answers on your paper.

1. permitted to do something
   a. forbidden
   b. allowed
   c. contained

2. a **foolish** rule
   a. law
   b. unusual
   c. silly

3. left the room **solo**
   a. alone
   b. allowed
   c. unhappy

4. forbidden to do something
   a. permitted
   b. photographed
   c. not allowed

Check your answers. You should have picked **b** for 1, **c** for 2, **a** for 3, and **c** for 4. If you didn't get those answers, read back through activities A and B.

Here are the eight new words in this lesson. Next to each new word is a word or phrase that has almost the same meaning. Look for the new words in the story below. Use the words with the same meaning to help you understand the lesson words.

transmit—send
accomplishment—deed
aloft—high up
observed—watched

employed—working
invented—made
limit — amount allowed
halted—stopped

Not-So-Famous Firsts

Every person likes to be first. The people named in this story each did something before anyone else did. You have probably never heard their names. Yet each person has a place in history.

Nathan B. Stubblefield was the first person to **transmit** his voice over radio. Stubblefield did not want anyone to steal his idea. He didn't tell anyone about his **accomplishment**. That is why he is not famous today.

Mary Walsh and Charles Colton wanted their wedding to be different. They got married while they were **aloft** in a balloon. No one had ever done that before. Their guests **observed** them from several hundred feet below.

Many people can thank George Crum for their favorite party food. Crum was **employed** as a cook at a hotel. In 1853, he **invented** the first potato chips.

Jacob German was probably not happy about being first to do something. In 1899, he became the first driver to be put in jail for going over the speed **limit**. He was **halted** by a policeman. He was going 12 miles per hour.

A. Here are the meanings of the new words in this lesson. Can you match the meanings with the lesson words? For help, reread the words or phrases on page 84 that had the same meanings. Also, look at the way the words were used in the story. Write down your matches.

1. send from one place to another
2. high in the air
3. the biggest amount allowed
4. brought to a stop
5. something important a person did
6. saw something happen
7. made something before anyone else
8. having a job

B. Look at the word in dark type in each item below. Decide which answer means almost the same as the word in dark type. Put your answers on your paper.

1. **transmit** a message
   a. write
   b. send
   c. listen to

2. go over a **limit**
   a. book
   b. cloud
   c. amount allowed

3. **invented** a machine
   a. made
   b. saw
   c. stopped

4. **halted** the fight
   a. started
   b. stopped
   c. won

C. Write a sentence to answer each question below. Use the lesson word in dark type in your sentence.

1. What was the best sports **accomplishment** this year?
2. What is the strangest thing you ever **observed**?
3. In what job would you like to be **employed**?

Here are the eight new words in this lesson. Next to each new word is a word or phrase that has almost the same meaning. Look for the new words in the story below. Use the words with the same meaning to help you understand the lesson words.

difficulty—trouble
organization—club
requirement—rule
currently—presently

females—women
festival—fair
events—happenings
contest—game

The Same Name

Do you ever have **difficulty** remembering someone's name? No one has that trouble in the Jim Smith Society.

The Jim Smith Society is a special **organization**. There is one **requirement** for joining the club. Your name has to be Jim Smith. **Currently** more than 1,150 people are in the club. A few of the Jim Smiths are **females**.

Every year the Jim Smith Society holds a big **festival** in Allenberry, Pennsylvania. One of the **events** of the festival is a softball game. Every player in the game is named Jim Smith. Even the umpire is named Jim Smith. It is easy to tell who is the best player in the **contest**. It is Jim Smith, of course.

A. Here are the meanings of the new words in this lesson. Can you match the meanings with the lesson words? For help, reread the words or phrases on page 86 that had the same meanings. Also, look at the way the words were used in the story. Write down your matches.

1. something you must do
2. a big party or fair
3. a game someone wins
4. a special group or club
5. at the present time
6. girls or women
7. things that happen
8. a problem or trouble

B. Look at the word in dark type in each item below. Decide which answer means almost the same as the word in dark type. Put your answers on your paper.

1. have **difficulty** with
   a. fun
   b. trouble
   c. party

2. special **events**
   a. happenings
   b. present
   c. people

3. a **female** president
   a. important
   b. woman
   c. great

4. a close **contest**
   a. near
   b. trouble
   c. game

C. Write a sentence to answer each question below. Use the lesson word in dark type in your sentence.

1. Which school **organization** do you belong to?
2. What is a **requirement** for joining one school club?
3. How many people are **currently** in your English class?

LESSON 3

Here are the eight new words in this lesson. Next to each new word is a word or phrase that has almost the same meaning. Look for the new words in the story below. Use the words with the same meaning to help you understand the lesson words.

homeland – birthplace
sponsored – organized
passport – document used for travel
maestro – master of an art

concerts – musical performances
spectators – people who watch
authorities – people in charge
composer – writer of music

Vladimir Horowitz Goes Home

He had fled Russia when he was twenty years old. Many years later, in April, 1986, the world famous pianist returned to his **homeland**. His tour and homecoming visit were **sponsored** by the U.S. and Russian governments.

Saying, "My face is my **passport**," Vladimir Horowitz was a very happy and proud Russian when he set foot on his native soil. He had come home to be a brother to his people and to share some precious musical moments with them. He brought his own piano and video tapes

of his favorite action and science-fiction movies.

The Soviet **authorities** gave him a chilly welcome. But the people greeted him warmly. They waited in long lines to get tickets to his piano **concerts**. He gave one concert in Moscow, the capital city of Russia, and another in Leningrad. Both concerts were sold out. Many people were not able to see him because they had no tickets. An audience of students was invited to watch a rehearsal. These student **spectators** cheered him wildly.

The **maestro** also visited relatives and friends. He had not seen them for sixty-one years! A Russian composer said, "I think Vladimir Horowitz will always remember his homecoming visit, and we will too."

A. Here are the meanings for the new words in this lesson. Can you match the meanings with the lesson words? For help, reread the words or phrases on page 88 that had the same meanings. Also, look at the way the words were used in the story. Write down your matches.

1. skilled musician
2. organized or set-up
3. musical performances
4. where a person is born
5. people in charge of things
6. one who writes music
7. a document used when you travel
8. people who watch an event

B. Read the beginning of each sentence below. Decide which ending is the best ending for the sentence. Put your answers on your paper.

1. A violin **maestro** is __ .
   a. a person who cannot play the violin
   b. a person who makes violins
   c. a person who plays the violin very well

2. The **authorities** are __ .
   a. people who follow someone else
   b. the people in charge
   c. the common people

3. **Spectators** __ .
   a. take part in games
   b. watch events
   c. only listen to football games

4. A **passport** is used __ .
   a. when you travel
   b. if you shop
   c. in Washington D.C.

C. Write a sentence to answer each question below. Use the lesson word in dark type in your sentence.

1. Do any of your favorite singers give **concerts**?
2. What did the **authorities** forbid you to do?
3. What are some American sports that are played in a stadium of **spectators**?

89

Here are the eight new words in this lesson. Next to each new word is a word or phrase that has almost the same meaning. Look for the new words in the story below. Use the words with the same meaning to help you understand the lesson words.

recent—new
journeyed—traveled
explorers—travelers
voyages—sea trips

records—writings
crew—team
settle—live
soil—ground

Who Really Discovered America?

For a long time, people believed that Christopher Columbus was the first person from Europe to land in the New World. But **recent** findings have shown that several other people may have **journeyed** to America long before Columbus.

One group of **explorers** who probably beat Columbus to America was the Vikings. They came from Northern Europe to Iceland and Greenland. They may have made **voyages** as far west as Canada more than 800 years ago. The Vikings did not leave any **records**. But Eskimo carvings made more than 800 years ago show people dressed the way the Vikings did.

The Vikings may not have been the first to come to America either. St. Brendan, an Irish monk, may have landed in Canada more than 1,200 years ago. Old writings show that the monk left Ireland in a leather boat. He had a small **crew** with him. Several years ago, a modern explorer sailed the same kind of boat from Ireland to Canada in 50 days. St. Brendan may have made the same trip. No one knows for sure.

Columbus may not have been first. He is the most important explorer, however. Why? Soon after Columbus' four trips, other explorers came to the New World. They decided to **settle** here. They set up new homes on American **soil**.

A. Here are the meanings of the new words in this lesson. Can you match the meanings with the lesson words? For help, reread the words or phrases on page 90 that had the same meanings. Also, look at the way the lesson words were used in the story. Write down your matches.

1. made a trip
2. live in one place
3. ideas written down
4. trips made on boats
5. a team of people who work together
6. ground, dirt, or land
7. new or modern
8. people who travel to new places

B. Read the beginning of each sentence below. Choose the answer that best completes the sentence. Put your answers on your paper.

1. Someone who wants to live in one place wants to __.
   a. travel
   b. settle
   c. record

2. A trip made on the sea is a __.
   a. crew
   b. traveler
   c. voyage

3. A new or modern event is __.
   a. recent
   b. old
   c. a record

4. *Ground* is another word for __.
   a. trip
   b. team
   c. soil

C. Write a sentence to answer each question below. Use the lesson word in dark type in your sentence.

1. What is the most interesting place you ever **journeyed** to?
2. What new place would you like to **explore**?
3. Where are student **records** kept in your school?

LESSON 5

Here are the eight new words in this lesson. Next to each new word is a word or phrase that has almost the same meaning. Look for the new words in the story below. Use the words with the same meaning to help you understand the lesson words.

physician—doctor
suffering—hurting
remove—take out
relieved—eased

remedy—cure
bulky—thick
pressure—weight
discomfort—pain

A New Cure

Several men came to Dr. Elmar Lutz, a New Jersey **physician**. They said they were **suffering** from pain in the lower part of their backs.

Dr. Lutz asked each man to **remove** his wallet. Then he asked them a question. He didn't ask for money. He asked, "How do you feel?" Each man said he felt much better. Taking out their wallets had **relieved** the pain. Dr. Lutz had found a **remedy** for their problem.

How can a wallet make a person's back hurt? Dr. Lutz said that many men carry **bulky** wallets in their hip pockets. The wallets are filled with money and credit cards. The credit cards are very stiff. A stiff wallet puts a lot of **pressure** on the nerves of the person's lower back. Taking out the wallet can end the **discomfort**.

Dr. Lutz doesn't make his patients take any money out of their wallets. He said he doesn't charge for his wallet remedy.

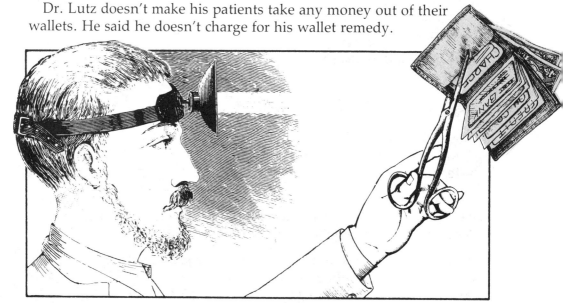

A. Here are the meanings of the new words in this lesson. Can you match the meanings with the lesson words? For help, reread the words or phrases on page 92 that had the same meanings. Also, look at the way the lesson words were used in the story. Write down your matches.

1. a person who treats sick people
2. a weight that pushes against something else
3. take out or take away
4. a painful feeling
5. having feelings of pain
6. something that cures a sickness
7. large or thick
8. made something easier

B. Look at each sentence below. Decide which answer is the best word to replace the word in italics. Put your answers on your paper.

1. The patient said she was *hurting* from a pain in her foot.
   a. suffering
   b. relieving
   c. removing

2. Doctors are still trying to find a *cure* for colds.
   a. physician
   b. pressure
   c. remedy

3. The acrobat found that standing on her head would *ease* her headache.
   a. suffer
   b. relieve
   c. experience

4. Some people feel *pain* in their knees on rainy days.
   a. relief
   b. discomfort
   c. bulky

C. Write a sentence to answer each question below. Use the lesson word in dark type in your sentence.

1. What was the worst **discomfort** you ever felt?
2. Why do some sick people put off going to a **physician**?
3. What do you think is the best **remedy** for a cold?

WORDS WITH OPPOSITE MEANINGS

Some words mean just the opposite of each other. You can use an opposite to explain the meaning of a new word. Here is an example. The words *sad* and *cheerful* are opposites. One way to explain the meaning of *cheerful* is to say it means *not sad*.

Three words are in dark type in the following short paragraph. Using opposites can help you tell the meanings of the new words.

Here are some more strange laws that have been passed. In Trenton, New Jersey, it is against the law to throw a **rotten** pickle onto the street. In Lexington, Kentucky, you are **prohibited** from carrying an ice-cream cone in your pocket. In Portland, Oregon, it is **improper** to wear roller skates in a public rest room.

Here are the three words in dark type and their opposites. Use the opposites to help you complete the sentences below the words. Put your answers on your paper.

rotten	good
prohibited	allowed
improper	right

1. If a pickle is not good, it is __.
2. If you are not allowed to do something, you are __ from doing it.
3. Another word for *not right* is __.

Do the following activities. You will learn more about using opposites to explain the meanings of words.

A. Read the paragraph on the next page about some more silly laws. Notice the words in dark type.

Peculiar laws have even been passed about horses. In Wilbur, Washington, any horse a person rides must be **attractive** to look at. A law in Ft. Lauderdale, Florida, says that riders must **attach** a horn and taillight to their horses. In Hillsboro, Oregon, it is **illegal**, or against the law, to let a horse ride in the back seat of your car. And in Marshalltown, Iowa, horses are **prohibited** from eating fire hydrants.

Read each incomplete sentence below. Decide which word above in dark type is the best one to complete the sentence. Put your answers on your paper.

1. *Ugly* is the opposite of __.
2. *Allowed* is the opposite of __.
3. *Lawful* is the opposite of __.
4. *Usual* is the opposite of __.
5. *Take off* is the opposite of __.

B. Look at each vocabulary test question below. Choose the answer that means the opposite of the word in dark type. Make sure you choose an opposite. Don't pick a word with the same meaning. Put your answers on your paper.

1. an **illegal** act
   a. improper
   b. lawful
   c. ugly

2. **attach** a small sign
   a. take off
   b. put on
   c. make

3. an **attractive** animal
   a. strange
   b. rotten
   c. ugly

4. **prohibited** from doing something
   a. not allowed
   b. allowed
   c. illegal

Here are the eight new words in this lesson. Next to each new word is a word or phrase that has almost the same meaning. Look for the new words in the story below. Use the words with the same meaning to help you understand the lesson words.

vicious—mean   **guide**—lead
escape—get away   **unfortunate**—unlucky
enormous—huge   **attack**—fight
locate—find   **damage**—harm

The World's Most Dangerous Army

This army is one of the most **vicious** in the world. No one knows where or when it will fight next. Nothing can **escape** from this army. The army has millions of soldiers. Yet none of the soldiers can see, hear, or speak. The soldiers are ants.

Army ants live in **enormous** camps in Africa, Asia, and Central America. A large army camp may have as many as 30 million ants.

Special ants, called scouts, go out first to **locate** food. They may find some big insects. They leave a smell to **guide** other ants to the food. Then the army strikes by surprise in lines up to 65 feet wide. The trapped animals can't get away. The **unfortunate** insects are carried back to feed all of the other hungry ants.

Army ants will eat any living thing. They usually eat other insects. But some army ants eat larger animals like horses and goats. Some ants even **attack** people.

Many people are happy when army ants come to their villages. Why? The ants eat field mice or other animals that **damage** people's homes or food. The ants clean out these harmful animals. When the ants move on, the people move back into their "clean" villages.

A. Each word or phrase below means the opposite of one of the new words listed at the top of the page. Can you write the new words and their opposites? For help, reread the words or phrases that had the same meaning. Also, look at the way the words were used in the story.

1. get caught   5. tiny
2. lucky   6. kind
3. follow   7. help
4. protect   8. lose

B. Choose the word or phrase that means the opposite of the word in dark type. Make sure you pick an opposite. Put your answers on your paper.

1. attack a village
   a. fight
   b. clean
   c. protect

2. a **vicious** animal
   a. mean
   b. kind
   c. blind

3. escape from prison
   a. get caught
   b. swim
   c. save

4. an **enormous** amount
   a. large
   b. tiny
   c. lucky

C. Write a sentence to answer each question below. Use the lesson word in dark type in your sentence.

1. Who is one **unfortunate** person you have read about?
2. In what parts of the world can you **locate** army ants?
3. What is one kind of insect that **damages** people's houses?

Here are the eight new words in this lesson. Next to each new word is a word or phrase that has almost the same meaning. Look for the new words in the story below. Use the words with the same meaning to help you understand the lesson words.

originated—started

restless—not relaxed

toss—throw

succeed—do well

suspended—hung up

rapid—fast

ascend—climb up

considerably—very much

The New Game

Very few people know how the game of basketball **originated**. Here is the true story.

James Naismith, a gym teacher at Springfield College, invented the game in 1891. Students at the school were **restless**. They wanted an exciting game to play inside during the winter.

Naismith decided to hang two wood boxes from sides of the gym. Players on one team would carry a soccer ball down the floor. They would try to **toss** the ball into the other team's box. Naismith sent a janitor to find boxes. The janitor did not **succeed** in locating boxes. Instead all he could find were two peach baskets. So the game was called "basket ball" and not "box ball."

Naismith **suspended** the baskets from a rail that went around the gym. The rail was ten feet high. Even today, a basket is ten feet high.

Students liked the game, but it was not **rapid** enough for them. After each goal, a player had to **ascend** a ladder and get the ball from the basket. Finally, someone thought of cutting out the bottom of the basket to let the ball go through.

Basketball has changed **considerably** since 1891. The first game was slow. It ended in a tie, 2–2. Today, games are very fast. Teams often score more than 100 points.

A. Each word or phrase below means the opposite of one of the new words listed on page 98. Can you write the new words and their opposites? For help, reread the words or phrases that had the same meaning. Also, look at the way the words were used in the story.

1. slow
2. very little
3. relaxed
4. ended
5. catch
6. pulled down
7. walk down
8. fail

B. Read the beginning of each sentence below. Decide which answer is the best ending for the sentence. Put your answers on your paper.

1. A restless person is not __.
   a. relaxed
   b. fast
   c. awake

2. If you don't ascend a ladder, you __.
   a. climb up it
   b. walk down it
   c. carry it

3. If you don't succeed, you __.
   a. catch something
   b. fail at something
   c. are quick

4. If you don't change considerably, you __.
   a. stay almost the same
   b. are restless
   c. are fast

C. Write a sentence to answer each question below. Use the lesson word in dark type in your sentence.

1. How far above the ground are the lights in your classroom **suspended**?
2. What is the best way to **toss** a basketball toward the basket?
3. When was the game of basketball **originated**?

Here are the eight new words in this lesson. Next to each new word is a word or phrase that has almost the same meaning. Look for the new words in the story below. Use the words with the same meaning to help you understand the lesson words.

totally—completely
scheduled—planned
opponents—rivals
victory—win

elevated—lifted
astounded—surprised
propelled—pushed forward
injured—hurt

The Flying Car

Race-car drivers are used to going at high speeds on the ground. But what do you do if your car **totally** leaves the ground? That is what happened to Bobby Johns. The flight that was not **scheduled** made him lose a big race.

Johns was leading the 1960 Daytona 500-mile race. He was far ahead of his **opponents.** There were only four miles to go. Everyone thought Johns would easily gain the **victory**.

Johns's car was going more than 150 miles an hour. Suddenly, the car was **elevated** off the ground. The car spun in the air and landed off the track. Everyone, including Johns, was **astounded**.

Here is what had happened. The pressure of the air had popped the back window out of Johns's fast-moving car. Wind rushed in through the wide opening. The force of the wind **propelled** the car through the air. The car sailed more than 60 feet before it came down and stopped.

Johns was not **injured**, but he was scared. He couldn't finish the race.

A. Each word or phrase below means the opposite of one of the new words listed on page 100. Can you write the new words and their opposites? For help, reread the words or phrases that had the same meaning. Also, look at the way the words were used in the story.

1. partly
2. dropped
3. teammates
4. unhurt
5. not surprised
6. unplanned
7. loss
8. pushed back

B. Look at each sentence below. Decide which answer is the opposite of the word in dark type in the sentence. Put your answers on your paper.

1. Three stops were **scheduled** on our bus trip.
   a. planned
   b. unplanned
   c. fun

2. The team was **astounded** to see 20,000 people at the game.
   a. unhappy
   b. not surprised
   c. angry

3. The boy used a rubber band to **propel** the paper airplane.
   a. move forward
   b. build
   c. push back

4. Several people were **injured** in the accident.
   a. caught
   b. unhurt
   c. hurt

C. Write a sentence to answer each question below. Use the lesson word in dark type in your sentence.

1. How much weight can you lift totally off the ground?
2. Which team is the best **opponent** your school will play in basketball?
3. Who gained the **victory** in the last election?

101

Sometimes two words sound the same but are spelled in different ways. The two words also have different meanings. *Sound-alikes* can cause some problems in reading and writing. You have to be careful to make sure you are using the right word.

Look at this paragraph about more strange laws. Two of the words are in dark type. The words are wrong. Each wrong word should have a sound-alike in its place. Do you know the right sound-alikes? Write your answers on your paper.

There are some funny laws about baths and bathtubs. An old Boston law says that a person can't take more than **won** bath a week. A Florida law says a person must wear **close** in a bathtub. A Virginia law says a bathtub can't be put inside a house. It must be put in the yard.

Check your answers. The words *won* and *one* are sound-alikes. So are the words *close* and *clothes*. The right words to use in the paragraph are **one** and **clothes.**

Some other words in the paragraph about laws also have sound-alikes. Look back at the paragraph. Can you find sound-alikes for the words *weak* and *where*? Write the sound-alikes on your paper.

Do the activities on the next page. You will learn more about using the right sound-alikes.

A. Here are six more pairs of sound-alikes and their meanings. The words sound the same, but they have different meanings and spellings.

aloud—out loud
allowed—permitted

ours—belonging to us
hours—times of the day

their—belonging to them
there—in that place

passed—agreed on or went by
past—time that has gone by

made—caused something to
  happen
maid—a woman servant

bawled—cried very loudly
bald—without any hair

Read the following paragraph about strange laws and barbers. Decide which sound-alikes are right in the paragraph. Put your answers on your paper.

In Waterloo, Nebraska, barbers are not **(aloud, allowed)** to eat onions during working **(ours, hours)**. In Elkhart, Indiana, barbers can't tell children they will cut off **(their, there)** ears if the children are bad. In Baton Rouge, Louisiana, a law was once **(passed, past)**. The law **(made, maid)** 25 cents the highest price a **(bawled, bald)** man must pay for a haircut.

B. For each question below, a definition is printed at the beginning. Choose the sentence in which the word in dark type has the same meaning as the definition given. Put your answers on your paper.

1. cried very loudly
  a. The baby **bawled** when her toy was lost.
  b. The **bald** man helped the baby look for the toy.

2. time that has gone by
  a. The winner **passed** the loser near the end of the race.
  b. We have learned many new words in the **past** two weeks.

LESSON 9

Here are the eight new words in this lesson and their meanings. Each word has a sound-alike that sometimes confuses readers. Look for the new words in the story below. Notice how they are used.

bare—empty or uncovered
whether—if
stare—look hard
guessed—imagined

feat—accomplishment
whole—complete
through—from one side to the other
lone—by itself

The Talking Head

You have come to see a magic show. The curtain opens. You see a table in front of you. The table is **bare**, except for a strange sight. In the middle of the table is a plate with a woman's head on it. You don't see her body. The head talks to you, but you don't know **whether** you should believe your eyes or ears. You **stare** at the table, looking for the woman's body. How could this be true? The answer is magic.

"The Talking Head" is a famous magic trick. Very few people have ever **guessed** how it works. Do you know how the magician has done this **feat**?

The secret is a mirror. The magician has put a mirror between one front leg of the table and one back leg. You think you can see the other back leg. But what you are seeing is a reflecton of a front leg. You think you are seeing a **whole** table, but you are seeing only half. A woman is kneeling behind the mirror. Her head sticks out **through** a hole in the table and the plate. You are not really seeing a **lone** head. The body is just blocked from your eyes.

A. Here are sound-alikes for each of the new words on page 104. Each sound-alike has a different spelling and meaning from the lesson word. Can you write a lesson word to match each sound-alike?

1. weather
2. hole
3. threw
4. loan
5. guest
6. bear
7. feet
8. stair

B. Read each sentence below. Decide which sound-alike should go in the blank. Put your answers on your paper.

1. The pitcher ___ the ball quickly to the catcher.
   a. threw
   b. through

2. The owner of the company went to the bank to ask for a ___.
   a. lone
   b. loan

3. Winning a race is a wonderful ___.
   a. feat
   b. feet

4. When we went camping, we were frightened by a ___.
   a. bare
   b. bear

C. Write a sentence to answer each question below. Use the lesson word in dark type in your sentence.

1. Are trees usually **bare** in the summer or winter?
2. How many halves are in a **whole** object?
3. If you had a **lone** nickel, how much money would you have?

LESSON 10

Here are the eight new words in this lesson and their meanings. Each word has a sound-alike that sometimes confuses readers. Look for the new words in the article below. Notice how the words are used.

their—belonging to them
piece—one part of something
weight—how heavy something is
bored—pushed or drilled
site—location

write—put words on paper
seller—someone who trades
  something for money
heir—person who is left something by someone who has died

Heavy Money

People on the island of Yap don't need wallets to carry **their** money. They need a big stick and strong arms. A **piece** of Yap money can be 12 feet high. It can have a **weight** of more than 2,000 pounds.

Yap coins are large round stones. A hole has been **bored** through the center of the stone. When people on Yap move, they roll the stone to the **site** of their new home.

People on Yap don't give or take any money when something is sold. Instead, they **write** down on the face of the stone coin what they bought or sold. Later on, the buyer will trade something back to the **seller**. That way, everything stays even.

When the leader of a Yap family dies, the family coin is passed on to the leader's **heir**. One coin can last many years.

A. Here are sound-alikes for each of the new words at the top of the page. Each sound-alike has a different spelling and meaning from the lesson word. Can you write a lesson word to match each sound-alike?

1. air
2. wait
3. sight
4. board

5. cellar
6. peace
7. there
8. right

B. For each question below, choose the sentence in which the word in dark type has the same meaning as the definition given.

1. how heavy something is
   a. The man went on a diet to lower his **weight**.
   b. The man had to **wait** 10 minutes for a train.

2. ability to see something
   a. Doctors helped the man get his **sight** back.
   b. The **site** of the new plant is near Smith Road.

3. pushed or drilled
   a. John made a bookshelf from an old **board**.
   b. John **bored** a hole into the wood.

4. part of a house below the ground.
   a. We stored our old clothes in the **cellar**.
   b. The **seller** of the old house is Mr. Moore.

C. Write a sentence to answer each question below. Use the lesson word in dark type in your sentence.

1. How many **pieces** of money are you carrying today?
2. What city is the **site** of the White House?
3. What would you use to **bore** a hole in a stone?

Choose the word or phrase that means the same, or almost the same, as the word in dark type. Put your answers on your answer sheet. The words in dark type come from Lessons 1–3.

Test Tips: Read the phrase with the word in dark type carefully. Decide if you have ever heard the word or phrase before. Use your past knowledge to help you pick the word that has almost the same meaning.

1. a big **organization**
   a. job
   b. club
   c. problem
   d. church organ

2. wild **spectators**
   a. animals
   b. fruits
   c. audience
   d. life

3. an important **accomplishment**
   a. person
   b. deed
   c. magazine
   d. event

4. hold a **festival**
   a. big party
   b. big meeting
   c. large balloon
   d. important job

5. school **authorities**
   a. people who listen
   b. people who make speeches
   c. children who follow rules
   d. people who take charge

6. **transmit** a message
   a. send
   b. read
   c. write
   d. make up

7. proud of his **homeland**
   a. place where one works
   b. place of learning
   c. place of origin
   d. place where one lives

8. be **employed**
   a. upset
   b. working
   c. leading
   d. dangerous

Choose the word or phrase that best completes each sentence. The key words in the sentences come from Lessons 4–5.

Test Tips: Read the beginning of the sentence carefully. Decide what word is the most important one in the sentence. This is the key word. Look for the answer that means the same as the key word.

1. Explorers try to find __.
   a. money
   b. jobs
   c. boats
   d. new places

2. People in a crew are part of the same __.
   a. family
   b. team
   c. friends
   d. party

3. A physician tries to __.
   a. cure sick people
   b. find new places
   c. look for money
   d. stop criminals

4. A recent event happened __.
   a. long ago
   b. not long ago
   c. last year
   d. next year

5. People who keep records __.
   a. write down information
   b. sing a lot
   c. like to travel
   d. stay in one place

6. Someone who is suffering is __.
   a. feeling happy
   b. feeling pain
   c. feeling alarm
   d. feeling sleepy

7. If a pain is relieved, it is __.
   a. stronger
   b. worse
   c. starting again
   d. weaker

8. A bulky wallet is __.
   a. empty
   b. thick
   c. dark
   d. small

Choose the word or phrase that is most nearly the opposite of the word in dark type. Put your answers on your answer sheet. The words in dark type come from Lessons 6–8.

Test Tips: Read all four answers carefully. Make sure you pick an opposite. Don't be tricked by a word with the same meaning or a word that looks like the word in dark type.

1. A **vicious** lion
   a. kind
   b. mean
   c. angry
   d. violent

2. **Propelled** by the wind
   a. sailed
   b. pushed forward
   c. pushed backward
   d. made cold

3. Started off **rapidly**
   a. readily
   b. slowly
   c. timely
   d. quickly

4. **Ascend** the stairs
   a. walk down
   b. send to
   c. slip on
   d. climb

5. **Enormous** person
   a. not normal
   b. large
   c. tiny
   d. unusual

6. A **scheduled** stop
   a. unplanned
   b. short
   c. bus
   d. quick

7. **Locate** your brother
   a. love
   b. lose
   c. stop
   d. find

8. **Astounded** by what she said
   a. not surprised
   b. surprised
   c. hurt
   d. not hurt

Choose the sentence in which the word in dark type means the same as the definition given. The words in dark type or their sound-alikes come from Lessons 9–10.

Test Tips: Try to put the definition in place of the word in dark type in each sentence. Then see which sentence makes sense. Don't be tricked by a sound-alike or by a word with a different meaning.

1. location
    a. What is the **site** of the new building?
    b. The man lost his **sight** in the accident.
    c. The hunter looked down the **sight** of his gun.

2. accomplishment
    a. A yard is three **feet.**
    b. Climbing a mountain is a great **feat.**
    c. The cat landed on its **feet.**

3. from one side to the other
    a. The man **threw** a rock at the store window.
    b. She left after she was **through** with the test.
    c. The magician seemed to walk **through** the wall.

4. pushed or drilled
    a. She was named to the school **board.**
    b. The man **bored** a hole in the wall.
    c. Watching the movie **bored** her.

5. not covered
    a. The trees were **bare.**
    b. A **bear** stole our food.
    c. The woman could not **bear** any more pain.

6. person left something by a person who dies
    a. The **air** was filled with smoke.
    b. I am my father's only **heir.**
    c. The man sang a lively **air.**

PART 2 *Context Clues*

In Part 2, you are going to learn a good way to guess what a new word means. You will learn to be a detective looking for meaning clues. You will learn to look carefully at how a word is used in a story. This will help you guess the word's meaning. Noticing the other words in a story will help you understand a new word.

Look at the picture below. The picture shows the meaning of the word *furious*. Use the picture as a clue. What do you think *furious* means?

Suppose you are reading a story. You come across a hard new word. How can you decide what the new word means?

One good way is to be a detective looking for clues to the word's meaning. Look at the words and sentences that come before and after the new word. The information around a new word is called its *context*. The meaning clues you find around a new word are called *context clues*.

Practice using context clues with the following strange but true sports story. One new word is in dark type. Can you find some context clues to help you guess what the word means?

Baseball pitcher Tony Freitas did something amazing. He once struck out a batter and caught the third strike himself. The ball **rebounded** off the catcher's chest protector. Freitas caught the ball as it came back toward him.

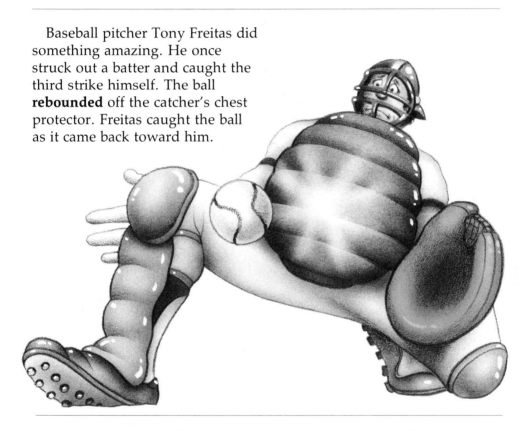

Check your answer. Think about what happened. The ball went toward the catcher. Then it came back to the pitcher. You can even see the words *came back* in the last sentence. All of these clues help you know that **rebounded** means *came back*.

You should look for several different kinds of context clues when you read. On the next two pages are four different kinds of clues to look for.

CLUE 1: DEFINITION CLUE

Sometimes you will find the meaning of a new word given right before or after the word. The meaning will be in the same sentence. Look for a definition clue in the following strange sports story. Use the clue to help you know what **existed** means.

Dr. Alain Bombard sailed a small boat all the way across the Atlantic Ocean. He didn't carry any food or water with him. He **existed**, or lived, for 65 days on sea water and fish he caught.

Check your answer. The words *or lived* come right after **existed**. The meaning of **existed** is given to you. It means *lived*.

CLUE 2: SAME MEANING CLUE

Sometimes you will find a word that has the same meaning as a new word. The word with the same meaning may come before or after the new word. It may be in another sentence. Look for a word that means the same as **remained** in the next strange sports story. Use the other word to help you know the meaning of *remained*.

In bowling, 300 is a perfect score. James T. Blackstone once bowled a 299½ score. How did he do it? On his last throw, one pin broke in half. Half of the pin **remained** standing. Because the half-pin stayed up, Blackstone did not make a perfect score.

Check your answer. You read that half a pin remained standing. You also read that half a pin stayed up. You can guess that **remained** probably means *stayed*.

CLUE 3: OPPOSITE CLUE

Sometimes you can find a word with an opposite meaning of a new word. The opposite may be in another sentence. The opposite will help you guess the meaning of the new word. Look for an opposite of **prior to** in the next strange sports story. Use the opposite to guess the meaning of **prior to**.

Sam Chapman once hit two home runs in two days. Yet he made both hits in the same game. He hit one home run **prior to** midnight. He hit the other home run after midnight.

Check your answer. The word *after* is an opposite of **prior to**. You can guess that **prior to** means *before*.

CLUE 4: EXPERIENCE CLUE

Sometimes you can guess the meaning of a new word because the meaning makes sense to you. The meaning fits with things you know to be true. Use your experience to guess the meaning of **error** in the next story.

Gary Pettit was once the high scorer for both teams in a basketball game. He scored 16 points for his team. He also made an **error** by putting in a basket for the other team. Gary's team won, 34–3.

Check your answer. You know that players don't usually try to score for the other team. So, Gary probably made the basket by mistake. You can guess that **error** means *mistake*.

Here are the eight new words in this lesson. Their meanings are not listed. Look for the words in the story below. Try to find context clues to help you guess the meanings. You will find some hints to help you in the first activity on page 117.

collect   destroy
profitable   rare
issued   accompanied
earliest   expensive

Get Rich with Baseball Cards

Thousands of people **collect** baseball cards. Some people save cards for fun. Some people collect cards for money. Some cards are worth a lot of money. Collecting baseball cards can be very **profitable**. Collectors can make a lot of money by selling their cards.

The first baseball cards came out in the 1880's. They were **issued**, or sent out, by tobacco companies. One of the **earliest** cards was of Honus Wagner of the Pittsburgh Pirates. Wagner did not smoke, and he did not want other people to smoke. He asked the tobacco company to **destroy** all of the cards with his picture on them. The company was able to tear up all but 14 cards. Those 14 cards are now very **rare**. They are each worth more than $12,000.

In 1933, bubble-gum companies decided to issue baseball cards. Baseball cards and bubble gum have **accompanied** each other since then. Today, more than 250 million bubble-gum cards are printed each year. What is the most **expensive** bubble-gum card? A 1952 Mickey Mantle card is the most costly. It can sell for as much as $3,000.

JIM BOTTOMLEY

URBAN (RED) FABER

A. Each question below gives you a hint about using context clues in the story you just read. The clues will help you understand the new words in the lesson. Use the hints to help you choose the best meaning for each word in dark type. Put your answers on your paper.

1. What word that means the same as **collect** is used in the next sentence of the story?
   a. save
   b. cards
   c. fun

2. Collecting baseball cards is **profitable** because you can ___.
   a. collect a lot
   b. make money
   c. play baseball better

3. The words after **issued** tell you that it means ___.
   a. company
   b. sent out
   c. collected

4. What word that means the same as **earliest** is used two sentences before in the story?
   a. sent out
   b. came out
   c. first

5. What phrase that means the same as **destroy** is used in the next sentence of the story?
   a. tear up
   b. smoke
   c. send out

6. Since there are only 14 Honus Wagner cards, you can guess that **rare** means ___.
   a. unusual
   b. nice
   c. beautiful

7. If gum and cards **accompanied** each other, they ___.
   a. collected
   b. saved
   c. went together

8. What word that means the same as **expensive** is used in the next sentence of the story?
   a. costly
   b. most
   c. card

B. Write a sentence to answer each question below. Use the lesson word in dark type in your sentence.

1. What is another **profitable** thing to collect?
2. What is the most **expensive** thing you own?
3. Who **accompanied** you to the first movie you ever saw?

117

Here are the eight new words in this lesson. Their meanings are not listed. Look for the words in the story below. Try to find context clues to help you guess the meanings. You will find some hints to help you in the first activity on page 119.

occur   role
purchase   conversations
assist   convict
honorable   depressed

He Couldn't Be Bought

This story sounds like something that might happen only on television. But it really did **occur**.

Edward Vaughan was not making much money as a policeman. He needed money to **purchase** things for his wife and six children. Mike Pellicci was a criminal in Vaughan's town. He wanted Vaughan to help him break the law. Pellicci promised to pay Vaughan well to **assist** him.

Vaughan decided it was more important to be **honorable**, or to do the right things. He told his police chief what had happened. The chief said Vaughan should pretend to help Pellicci. No one was to know about the **role** Vaughan was going to play.

Pellicci believed Vaughan's act. Pellicci made Vaughan be there when he talked with other criminals. Pellicci wanted to show his friends that he had "bought" a policeman. Vaughan wore a tape recorder under his clothes at these talks. He taped **conversations** the criminals had. Later, Vaughan played these tapes at Pellicci's trial. They helped to **convict** the criminal and get him sent to jail.

When Pellicci was arrested, the whole story of Vaughan's acting was told on the news. Vaughan's children had been **depressed** when they thought their father was helping a criminal. Now they were happy. They gave him a big welcome-home party that night.

A. Each question below gives you a hint about using context clues in the story you just read. The clues will help you understand the new words in the lesson. Use the hints to help you choose the best meaning for each word in dark type. Put your answers on your paper.

1. What word that means the same as **occur** is used in the sentence before in the story?
   a. sounds
   b. might
   c. happen

2. If you use money to **purchase** things, you know **purchase** means ___.
   a. buy something
   b. see something
   c. find something

3. What word that means the same as **assist** is used in the sentence before?
   a. wanted
   b. help
   c. break

4. The words after **honorable** tell you it means ___ .
   a. tell what happened
   b. be rich
   c. doing the right things

5. From experience, you know that an actor's **role** is a ___.
   a. part
   b. turn
   c. help

6. What word that means the same as **conversations** is used in the sentence before?
   a. clothes
   b. talks
   c. recorders

7. If a person goes to jail after being convicted, you know **convict** means ___.
   a. free
   b. find guilty
   c. play tapes

8. If *happy* is the opposite of **depressed**, you know **depressed** means ___.
   a. happy
   b. little
   c. unhappy

B. Write a sentence to answer each question below. Use the lesson word in dark type in your sentence.

1. What would you **purchase** first if you won a lot of money?
2. What is one way that police often **assist** people in a town?
3. With what famous person would you like to have a **conversation** today?

Here are the eight new words in this lesson. Their meanings are not listed. Look for the words in the story at the bottom of this page. Try to find context clues to help you guess the meanings. You will find some hints to help you in the first activity on page 121.

ordinary	displeased
communicate	constructed
instruct	term
emotions	exhausted

Animals That Talk

Lucy and Washoe were not **ordinary** students. They were special. They learned to use the same sign language that deaf people use to "talk." They used their hands to **communicate** with their teachers. What is so special about this story? Lucy and Washoe were not humans. They were chimps.

Several years ago, two teachers decided to **instruct** chimps to use sign language. They began with Washoe. Washoe soon learned several words. She learned to ask questions. She would say, "Give me sweet, eat, please?"

Washoe learned to use signs to show **emotions**, or feelings. She learned that the sign for *dirty* meant something with dirt on it. One day she became **displeased** with her trainer. She signed, "Dirty Jack! You give me eat!" No one had taught her to use *dirty* in that way.

Washoe even **constructed** her own words. One day she saw a duck. She made the signs for *water* and *bird* together. She had made her own **term** for *duck.*

Roger Fouts, another teacher, began working with Lucy. She soon learned more than 150 words. Sometimes Lucy became **exhausted** from working hard. Then she would sign, "Roger tickle Lucy," or "Roger hug Lucy."

Washoe and Lucy taught people a lot about animals. Now people know that animals have feelings. Animals can also make up their own ideas.

A. Each question below gives you a hint about using context clues in the story you just read. The clues will help you understand the new words in this lesson. Use the hints to help you choose the best meaning for each word in dark type. Put your answers on your paper.

1. If *special* is the opposite of **ordinary**, you know that **ordinary** means __.
   a. not smart
   b. not special
   c. special

2. What word that means the same as **communicate** is used in the sentence before in the story?
   a. talk
   b. language
   c. learned

3. From your experience about what teachers do, you can guess that **instruct** means __.
   a. learn
   b. watch
   c. teach

4. The words right after **emotions** in the story help you know that it means __.
   a. feelings
   b. signs
   c. dirt

5. If Washoe called Jack "dirty" because she was displeased with him, **displeased** must mean __.
   a. happy
   b. angry
   c. kind

6. What word that means the same as **constructed** is used three sentences later?
   a. saw
   b. together
   c. made

7. What word that means the same as **terms** is used three sentences before?
   a. words
   b. constructed
   c. duck

8. If Lucy became exhausted from working hard, **exhausted** must mean __.
   a. happy
   b. tired
   c. smart

B. Write a sentence to answer each question below. Use the lesson word in dark type in your sentence.

1. Why do deaf people use their hands to **communicate**?
2. What is one thing you **instructed** an animal to do?
3. What kind of hard work makes you feel **exhausted**?

Here are the eight new words in this lesson. Their meanings are not listed. Look for the words in the story below. Try to find context clues to help you guess the meanings. You will find some hints to help you in the first activity on page 123.

capture	**security**
wealth	**gale**
risky	**cargo**
escorted	**amazing**

The Richest Cargo

In June, 1940, the German army took over Paris, France. English leaders were afraid that Germany would attack England next. They were also afraid that the Germans would **capture** the gold and money stored in English banks. The English leaders did not want Germany to take England's **wealth**.

The English decided to try something very dangerous. They would send more than seven billion dollars in gold and money by ship to Canada! This plan was very **risky** because German ships sailed near England. The German ships often sank English ships. The English didn't want their money to end up at the bottom of the ocean.

During July, August, and September, English ships filled with heavy loads of gold sailed to Canada. English war ships **escorted** the ships. The war ships went with them to give **security** against the German navy.

Several of the ships ran into problems. One was caught in a **gale**, a storm with very strong winds. Another was trapped in a very thick fog. The ship almost ran into an iceberg.

At last, all of the ships arrived safely in Canada. The rich **cargo** each ship carried was sent by train to Montreal. There it was stored in a special building until the war was over.

One thing was **amazing** about this story. During the three months, German boats sank 134 ships. But not one of the gold-carrying ships went down.

A. Each question below gives you a hint about using context clues in the story you just read. The clues will help you understand the new words in this lesson. Use the hints to help you choose the best meaning for each word in dark type. Put your answers on your paper.

1. What word that means the same as **capture** is used in the next sentence of the story?
   a. attack
   b. take
   c. be afraid

2. If England's wealth was its gold and money, you can guess that **wealth** means ___.
   a. poorness
   b. riches
   c. ships

3. What word that means the same as **risky** is used two sentences before?
   a. decided
   b. easy
   c. dangerous

4. What phrase that means the same as **escorted** is used in the next sentence?
   a. went with
   b. filled
   c. sailed

5. From your experience, you can guess that if war ships give **security**, they must give ___.
   a. money
   b. protection
   c. friends

6. The words right after **gale** help you know that it means ___.
   a. a storm with strong winds
   b. a problem
   c. an iceberg

7. Since you know that the ships carried cargo, you can guess that **cargo** means ___.
   a. a load of things
   b. ships
   c. building

8. By thinking about what happened in the story you can guess that **amazing** must mean ___.
   a. happy
   b. dangerous
   c. surprising

B. Write a sentence to answer each question below. Use the lesson word in dark type in your sentence.

1. Why is it **risky** to send money by ship across the ocean?
2. How is a **gale** different from a usual rain storm?
3. How can a war ship give **security** for a cargo ship?

Here are the eight new words in this lesson. Their meanings are not listed. Look for the words in the story below. Try to find context clues to guess the meanings. You will find hints to help you in the first activity on page 125.

tomb	**tradition**
archaeologist	**exterminated**
valuable	**ancient**
preserved	**perished**

King Tut's Curse

In 1922, a man named Howard Carter found the **tomb** of King Tut. Tut had been the king of Egypt thousands of years ago. Carter was an **archaeologist**, a person who studies very old things.

Carter found gold, diamonds, and other **valuable** things in the tomb. He also found the **preserved** body of King Tut. It had been kept in good shape for a long time.

Carter also found out about King Tut's curse. A curse is a strong wish that bad things will happen to someone. According to **tradition**, or very old beliefs, a curse protected King Tut. A person who touched anything in his tomb was supposed to be **exterminated**, or killed.

Carter did not believe in the curse. Carter and a rich man named George Herbert found the **ancient** tomb. It was hidden far below the ground.

Inside the tomb, Herbert was bitten by a mosquito. He died a month later. When he died all the lights in Cairo went out. No one knew why. Thousands of miles away, Herbert's dog also **perished** at almost the same time. Carter's own canary died when it was bitten by a cobra. A cobra is a snake that is supposed to protect Egypt's kings.

Later, two more men who worked in the tomb died suddenly. Carter said they did not die because of the curse. Many people didn't agree with him. Was there really a curse? No one knows for sure.

A. Each question below gives a hint about using context clues in the story you just read. The clues will help you understand the new words in this lesson. Use the hints to help you choose the best meaning for each word in dark type. Put your answers on your paper.

1. Since King Tut had died, his **tomb** must be his ___.
   a. home
   b. burying place
   c. richness

2. The words after **archaeologist** help you know that it means a person who ___.
   a. is very old
   b. likes Egypt
   c. studies old things

3. What you know about gold and diamonds helps you know that **valuable** means ___.
   a. worth a lot
   b. beautiful
   c. interesting

4. What phrase in the next sentence of the story has the same meaning as **preserved**?
   a. long time
   b. kept in good shape
   c. had been

5. The words after **tradition** help you know that it means ___.
   a. curse
   b. bad things
   c. very old beliefs

6. The words after **exterminated** help you know it means ___.
   a. happy
   b. killed
   c. cursed

7. Since you know that Tut died a long time ago, you can guess that **ancient** means ___.
   a. very old
   b. dead
   c. beautiful

8. What word that means the same as **perished** is used two sentences before?
   a. knew
   b. went out
   c. died

B. Write a sentence to answer each question below. Use the lesson word in dark type in your sentence.

1. What are some things an **archaeologist** might study?
2. What is one **ancient** place you have studied about in school?
3. What is the most **valuable** thing you own?

Choose the word or phrase that means the same, or almost the same, as the word in dark type. Put your answers on your answer sheet. The words in dark type come from Lessons 1–3.

Test Tips: Some answer choices are put in a test to trick you. Make sure you pick a word that means the same as the word in dark type. Don't pick an answer that fits in the phrase but does not have the same meaning as the word in dark type.

1. A **profitable** hobby
   a. fun
   b. enjoyable
   c. money-making
   d. dangerous

2. **Communicate** with a friend
   a. talk
   b. walk
   c. visit
   d. learn

3. Feel **depressed**
   a. deeply
   b. beautiful
   c. happy
   d. unhappy

4. **Constructed** a house
   a. owned
   b. bought
   c. sold
   d. made

5. A **rare** sight
   a. unusual
   b. exciting
   c. ugly
   d. expensive

6. **Assist** a friend
   a. answer
   b. talk to
   c. meet
   d. help

7. Become **exhausted**
   a. unhappy
   b. rich
   c. tired
   d. depressed

8. **Purchase** a house
   a. own
   b. buy
   c. sold
   d. build

Choose the word or phrase that means the same, or almost the same, as the word in dark type. The words in dark type come from Lessons 4–5.

Test Tips: Use the sentence context to help you. Try to put your answer choice in place of the word in dark type. Decide if the sentence still has the same meaning.

1. Skating on thin ice is a very **risky** thing to do.
   a. enjoyable
   b. dangerous
   c. sad
   d. silly

2. The boat sank during the **gale**.
   a. night
   b. voyage
   c. storm
   d. water

3. I discovered an **ancient** bone near my house.
   a. unusual
   b. expensive
   c. animal
   d. very old

4. Meat is **preserved** when it is frozen.
   a. kept in good shape
   b. made cold
   c. made a different color
   d. made bad

5. The man stored his **wealth** in a deep hole.
   a. old things
   b. old clothes
   c. cargo
   d. riches

6. My aunt **perished** last month after a car accident.
   a. got well
   b. died
   c. was hurt
   d. was alone

7. The boy's mother **escorted** him to school.
   a. sent
   b. left
   c. taught
   d. went with

8. Some people buy dogs to give them **security.**
   a. help
   b. cures
   c. love
   d. protection

PART 3 # Words with Several Meanings

In Part 3, you are going to learn more new words. Each new word can have several different meanings. You will practice using context clues again. The clues will help you decide which meaning of the word fits in the story you are reading.

Look at the four pictures below. Each picture shows a different meaning of one word. Can you guess what the secret word is? Do you know all four meanings of the word?

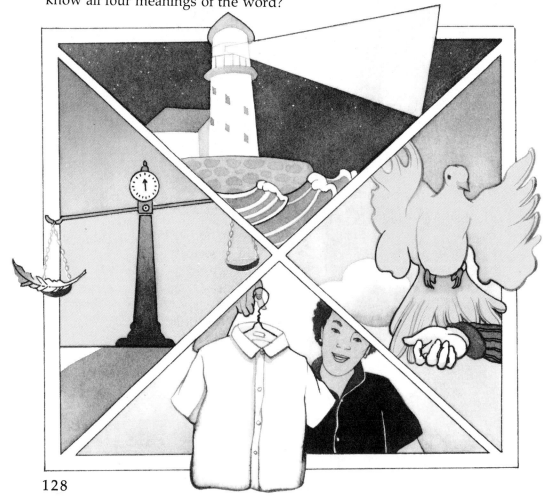

One word can have several different meanings. You need to look at the way the word is used in a sentence you are reading. That will help you know which meaning of the word fits in the sentence.

Look at these four sentences. The word **fall** is in each one. In each sentence, **fall** has a different meaning.

1. I love to walk through a forest in the **fall**.
2. Leaves of many different colors **fall** to the ground.
3. October 29 will **fall** on a Saturday this year.
4. The Lions will **fall** to our football team on October 29.

Here are four different meanings of *fall*. Each meaning fits the way *fall* is used in one of the sentences you just read. Match the meanings with the sentences they fit. Put your answers on your paper.

a. lose
b. drop down
c. the season after summer
d. happen or occur

Check your answers. Look at the way *fall* is used in each sentence. The correct matches are: 1. **c**, 2. **b**, 3. **d**, 4. **a**.

How many different meanings can you think of for each of the following words?

change
back
bowl
ring
trunk
store
yard
swallow

Do the activities on the next two pages. You will learn more about choosing the meaning of a word that fits in the reading.

A. Read the following paragraph. Look at the way **peck** is used in the paragraph. Try to decide what **peck** means.

Some people like to make up funny sentences. The sentences are hard to say out loud. That is why the sentences are called *tongue twisters.* Here is a famous tongue twister. "Peter Piper picked a **peck** of pickled peppers." Can you say the sentence out loud quickly three times in a row?

Here are four different meanings of **peck**. Which one fits the way the word was used in the tongue twister?

1. pick at something with a beak
2. a short, quick kiss
3. eat with small bites
4. amount of something, one-fourth of a bushel

Check your answer. The meaning that fits the tongue twister is **4**.

B. One word is in dark type in each tongue twister below. Decide which meaning listed below the tongue twister fits the way the word in dark type is used. Put your answers on your paper.

1. The **drain** in the train dripped again and again.
   a. a pipe through which water can run out
   b. use up

2. Rupert was **rash** to wrestle with Robin.

    a. reckless or not thinking

    b. red bumps on the skin

3. Miss Wiss lisps as she talks, and she **lists** as she walks.

    a. write things down in a row

    b. leans to one side

4. Penelope Pringle printed paragraphs on a **press**.

    a. push against something

    b. a machine for printing

Check your answers. You should have picked **a** for 1, **a** for 2, **b** for 3 and **b** for 4.

C. Here are the kinds of questions you sometimes see on a reading test. Read the meaning printed at the top of each question. Then find the sentence in which the word in dark type has the same meaning. Put your answers on your paper.

1. limit

    a. My father put a **curb** on how much money I could spend.

    b. The woman slipped as she walked off the **curb**.

2. very weak

    a. Her voice was so **faint** I could hardly hear her.

    b. The sun was so hot, I thought I was going to **faint**.

3. not very important

    a. Because Alice is a **minor**, she is not allowed to vote.

    b. I almost failed my driving test because of a **minor** mistake.

4. move quickly

    a. A seal can **dart** through the water.

    b. My **dart** landed in the middle of the target board.

5. place where people pray

    a. We visited a beautiful **temple** on our trip.

    b. Blood was coming out of the man's **temple**.

6. a made-up story

    a. The cat was playing with the orange **yarn**.

    b. My grandfather told me a **yarn** that was hard to believe.

Check your answers. You should have picked **a** for 1, **a** for 2, **b** for 3, **a** for 4, **a** for 5, and **b** for 6.

Here are the eight new words in this lesson. Their meanings are not listed. Each new word has several different meanings. Look for each word in the story. Use context clues to help you guess the meaning that fits in the story.

base	cutter
plot	scene
area	craft
object	current

Lost in the Bermuda Triangle

Find Florida on a map. Then locate the islands of Bermuda and Puerto Rico. Draw a line from the **base** of Florida to Bermuda to Puerto Rico and back to Florida. You will **plot** a triangle. The part of ocean inside is known as the Bermuda Triangle.

The Bermuda Triangle is a strange **area**. It frightens many people who fly or sail through it. About 100 airplanes or boats have disappeared there.

Here are just a few of the mysteries.

In 1945, five U.S. Navy planes flew out from Florida. They all disappeared. A boat was sent out. Its **object** was to find the planes. No one ever saw the boat or its 13-man crew again.

In 1967, a boat called the *Witchcraft* left Miami. At 9 p.m. the captain said his boat had hit something. It took only 15 minutes for a Coast Guard **cutter** to get to where the captain said he was. All the cutter found at the **scene** was empty water. Divers went under the water. They found nothing there either.

In 1978, another U.S. Navy plane disappeared while coming in for a normal landing. It has never been found.

What is behind these mysteries? Some people say that creatures from another planet live in the Bermuda Triangle. They shoot down the planes and boats. Scientists don't agree. They say that strong winds and storms in the area bring down the different **craft**. They also say the water **current** is very strong there. A boat that sinks can be carried far away before divers go down to look for it.

One expert says that strange things are still happening in the Bermuda Triangle.

A. Each of the words in Lesson 1 is listed below. After each one are two of its meanings. Decide which meaning fits the way the word was used in the story on page 132. Put your answers on your paper.

1. base
    a. the bottom of something
    b. build something on

2. plot
    a. make a secret plan
    b. mark a line on a map

3. area
    a. a place
    b. in math, an amount of space

4. object
    a. a thing
    b. a goal or purpose

5. cutter
    a. someone who divides something
    b. a small, fast boat

6. scene
    a. spot where something happens
    b. a part of a play

7. craft
    a. something handmade
    b. boat or airplane

8. current
    a. recent or up-to-date
    b. movement of air or water

B. The words below mean the same as four new words in this lesson. Match each word below with a lesson word. Write down your matches.

1. purpose
2. airplane
3. place
4. bottom

C. Write a sentence to answer each question below. Use the lesson word in dark type in your sentence.

1. What part of a tree is at its **base**, the branches or roots?
2. Who uses **cutters**, the Army or Coast Guard?
3. How can water **current** help a boat go faster?

Here are the eight new words in this lesson. Their meanings are not listed. Each new word has several different meanings. Look for each word in the story. Use context clues to help you guess the meaning that fits in the story.

steers   struck
recover   accept
star   entered
banner   root

Rodeo Champion

It was not easy for Clarence LeBlanc to become a rodeo champion. He had to show that he could rope **steers** faster than other cowboys. He had to prove that he could **recover** fully from a bad accident. He had to show that a black person could be a rodeo **star**.

Very few rodeo cowboys are black. But Clarence is one of the best stars of all. In 1980, he earned more than $28,000 in just four months. It was a **banner** year for him. Then bad luck **struck**.

One day Clarence was driving with some other cowboys. A car in front of them lost a tire. Clarence and his friends stopped to help. Suddenly, another car coming down the road lost control. It crashed into Clarence, crushing his leg. Doctors thought he might lose the leg. They said he would never be in another rodeo. Clarence didn't **accept** what they said. He was out of the hospital in one month. Within three months he was riding a bicycle 50 miles a day. His leg got stronger.

In January, 1981, he began competing in rodeos again. He **entered** a big rodeo in Tulsa. Everyone began to **root** for him. A steer was let loose. Clarence rode his horse after the steer. He roped the steer and wrestled it to the ground. He did it faster than anyone else. Clarence LeBlanc had proved he was a champion.

A. Each of the words in Lesson 2 is listed below. After each one are two of its meanings. Decide which meaning fits the way the word was used in the story on page 134. Put your answers on your paper.

1. **steers**
   a. directs or guides something
   b. male cattle

2. **recover**
   a. put a lid back on
   b. get well

3. **star**
   a. very good actor or athlete
   b. a large body in the sky

4. **banner**
   a. very good or excellent
   b. a flag

5. **struck**
   a. stopped working to get better work conditions
   b. happened or hit

6. **accept**
   a. get something
   b. believe or agree with

7. **entered**
   a. joined in
   b. went inside

8. **root**
   a. cheer for or want someone to win
   b. part of a plant below the ground

B. The words below mean the same as four new words in this lesson. Match each word below with a lesson word. Write down your matches.

1. hit
2. believe

3. cattle
4. excellent

C. Write a sentence to answer each question below. Use the lesson word in dark type in your sentence.

1. What baseball team do you usually **root** for? Why?
2. What was one contest that you **entered** recently?
3. How long does it usually take you to **recover** from a cold?

Here are the eight new words in this lesson. Their meanings are not listed. Each new word has several different meanings. Look for each word in the story. Use context clues to help you guess the meaning that fits in the story.

structure
furnish
supply
solution

reflects
switch
floor
operate

Wasting Energy

Every day, New York's World Trade Center uses as much electricity as the whole city of Schenectady, New York. The huge **structure** is a big waster of energy.

Office buildings waste millions of dollars' worth of oil every year. Why? The buildings have hundreds of windows. But the windows can't be opened. Machines must **furnish** all heating and cooling. Many days, people would be just as comfortable if the windows were open. Then the buildings would use less of the country's energy **supply**.

The glass used for windows also wastes energy. Most office windows are only one pane of glass. In winter, heat can leak out, and cold air can come in. One **solution** is to use double windows.

In summer, single windows let heat inside. One way to stop this is to use special glass. The glass **reflects** the sun's heat.

Office lights are another energy waster. In many buildings one **switch** turns on many different lights. Suppose one person needs to work late. Lighting one office may mean lighting a whole **floor**. The answer is to put in more switches.

Good planning may help save energy and money. A well-planned building may cost more to build. But it will cost less to **operate**. This may save money in the long run.

A. Each of the words in Lesson 3 is listed below. After each one are two of its meanings. Decide which meaning fits the way the word was used in the story on page 136. Put your answers on your paper.

1. structure
   a. a building
   b. the way something is put together

2. furnish
   a. buy furniture for
   b. give or provide

3. supply
   a. give or provide
   b. something which is stored up to be used later

4. solution
   a. a mixture
   b. an answer

5. reflects
   a. throws or sends back
   b. thinks deeply

6. switch
   a. change
   b. something that turns a machine on or off

7. floor
   a. the bottom of a room
   b. all parts of a building at the same height

8. operate
   a. use or run
   b. cut someone open to help cure them

B. The words or phrases below mean the same as four lesson words. Match each word or phrase with a lesson word. Write down your matches.

1. answer
2. throws back

3. use
4. building

C. Write a sentence to answer each question below. Use the lesson word in dark type in your sentence.

1. What is the largest **structure** in your town?
2. What are some machines that you know how to **operate**?
3. Why should buildings use glass that **reflects** the sun's heat?

TAKING TESTS

Choose the word or phrase that means the same, or almost the same, as the word in dark type. Put your answers on your answer sheet.

Test Tips: Remember that some words have several different meanings. Think of the different meanings of the word in dark type. Look for one of the meanings in the list of answers.

1. **Plot** a crime
   a. stop
   b. read about
   c. plan
   d. rob

2. **Recover** completely
   a. get well
   b. lose
   c. end
   d. forget

3. A **banner** year
   a. hot
   b. very good
   c. dry
   d. windy

4. **Switch** sides
   a. turn on
   b. fall on
   c. swing
   d. change

5. A **current** magazine
   a. recent
   b. water
   c. correct
   d. interesting

6. A big **structure**
   a. waste
   b. street
   c. building
   d. person

7. **Entered** the contest
   a. won
   b. lost
   c. joined in
   d. turned

8. **Furnish** an answer
   a. remember
   b. give
   c. forget
   d. ask

Choose the sentence in which the word in dark type means the same as the definition given.

Test Tips: Remember that the same word can have several different meanings. Look at the way the word in dark type is used in each sentence. Pick the sentence in which the word in dark type means the same as the definition given.

1. mixture
   a. The scientist put together a **solution** of powder and water.
   b. What is the **solution** to the third problem?
   c. I failed the test because I didn't know the right **solution**.

2. run or use
   a. The doctor had to **operate** to save the man's life.
   b. Yesterday I learned how to **operate** a computer.
   c. The phone was answered by the **operator**.

3. airplanes or boats
   a. I bought an interesting **craft** at the school art fair.
   b. Helen learned how to **craft** things out of clay.
   c. We saw several large **craft** coming toward the city.

4. bottom
   a. the **base** of the lamp is made of silver.
   b. The plane landed at the air **base**.
   c. The player ran toward third **base**.

5. goals or purposes
   a. My father **objects** to the way I dress for school.
   b. Her **objects** in taking the class were to learn and to make money.
   c. She held several beautiful **objects** in her hands.

6. movement of air or water
   a. I bought several **current** magazines at the store.
   b. What **current** events are you going to talk about?
   c. The strong ocean **current** took the boat out to sea.

PART 4 *Word Parts*

In Part 4, you are going to learn another good way to guess what a new word means. Sometimes part of a new word will be a word you already know. You will learn to look for word parts. You will also learn to use the word part as a clue to the meaning of a new word.

Look at the two pictures below. One picture shows the meaning of the word *downpour*. The other picture shows the meaning of the word *shipwreck*. Can you match each word with the right picture? Can you guess the meaning of each new word?

140

Sometimes you will see a new word in your reading or on a vocabulary test. You notice that a word you already know is in the new word. Many times you can use that word to help you guess what the new word means. This trick does not always work. But it can help you sometimes.

Read the following paragraph about a strange kind of tricycle. Two words are in dark type in the paragraph. Use parts of each new word to help you guess its meaning.

A special tricycle has been invented for lazy riders. It is called a sailing tricycle. It has pedals like other tricycles. It also has a large sail. If riders become **footsore**, they can unroll the sail. The **windblown** sail will push the tricycle forward.

1. What words do you see in **footsore**? Those words can help you guess that **footsore** means ___.
   a. having feet that hurt
   b. having feet that move fast

2. What words do you see in **windblown**? Those words can help you guess that **windblown** means ___.
   a. stopped by the wind
   b. pushed by the wind

Check your answers. The correct answers are **a** for 1 and **b** for 2.

Do the activities on the next two pages. You will learn more about using word parts to help you guess a new word's meaning.

A. Look at the words in List 1 below. Try to find a word you already know inside each new word. Then look at the meanings in List 2. Can you match each word with its meaning? Put your answers on your paper.

LIST 1
1. equality
2. evergreen
3. nightfall
4. lowland
5. warfare

LIST 2
a. tree that stays green all year
b. low and flat country
c. sameness or equalness
d. fighting
e. the beginning of evening

B. Read the following paragraph about another strange bicycle. Look for word parts in the words in dark type. Then answer the questions below the paragraph. Put your answers on your paper.

A strange looking bicycle you often see in old pictures is called a *penny farthing.* It is also called the *bone shaker.* It got this **nickname** because it gives a **troublesome** ride. The bike has an **outsized** front wheel, about four feet tall. The back wheel is very small. Some people still ride these bikes just for fun. It would be too **painful** to ride them very far.

1. Which word means *causing many problems?*
2. Which word means *bigger than usual?*
3. Which word means *filled with pain?*
4. Which word means *a special name something is called?*

Check your answers. 1. troublesome; 2. outsized; 3. painful; 4. nickname

142

C. Here are the kinds of questions you sometimes see on reading tests. Read the beginning of each sentence. Then find the answer that best completes the sentence. Use word parts to help you choose your answers. Put your answers on your paper.

1. The endpoint of a race is the place where it ___.
   a. starts
   b. finishes
   c. turns

2. If a boat is sailing midstream on a river it is ___.
   a. on the right side
   b. on the left side
   c. in the middle

3. If one team outnumbers the other it has ___.
   a. fewer players
   b. more players
   c. the same number of players

4. A hydroelectric plant helps to make ___.
   a. electricity
   b. oil
   c. gasoline

5. One of the westernmost states in the U.S. is ___.
   a. New York
   b. Illinois
   c. California

6. If a house is fireproof it should ___.
   a. not burn down
   b. burn down easily
   c. be on fire

Check your answers. You should have picked **b** for 1, **c** for 2, **b** for 3, **a** for 4, **c** for 5, and **a** for 6.

Here are the eight new words in this lesson. Their meanings are not listed. Notice how the words are used in the story below. Look for a word you know in each new word. The words inside will help you guess the meanings of the new words.

growth　　　　　　　　　**cleanliness**
skyscrapers　　　　　　　**shortage**
newcomers　　　　　　　**livelihood**
mountainous　　　　　　**overnight**

The World's Largest City

What was one of the world's largest cities in the year 1500? What city's **growth** is the fastest in the world today? What city will be the world's largest by the year 2000? The answer to all three questions is Mexico City.

Mexico City is two cities in one. Inside are beautiful old buildings and tall new **skyscrapers**. On the outside are rows of small ugly shacks. Millions of poor people live in these shacks.

Right now Mexico City has almost 15 million people. By the year 2000, over 30 million people will live there. More than 1,000 **newcomers** arrive every day. Many of these people were once farmers. They were not able to grow enough food in the **mountainous** areas where they lived. They decided to move to Mexico City.

These people find many problems in the big city. One problem is the lack of **cleanliness**. Some parts of the city are very dirty. Garbage is left in the streets. The garbage causes many people to get sick or die.

A **shortage** of houses and jobs causes other problems. Many people have to crowd together in the same shacks. They also can't find jobs to help them earn a **livelihood**.

Mexico City is trying to solve its problems. The solutions will not come **overnight**. But soon Mexico City hopes to be the biggest and the best city in the world.

144

A. Look for words you already know in the new words on page 144. The words inside will help you pick the best meanings in the questions below. Put your answers on your paper.

1. What word do you see inside **growth**? That word will help you guess that **growth** means ___.
   a. getting bigger
   b. getting smaller
   c. rowing a boat

2. What word do you see inside **skyscrapers**? That word helps you guess that **skyscrapers** are ___.
   a. small houses
   b. very tall buildings
   c. garbage scraps

3. What words do you see inside **newcomers**? Those words help you guess that **newcomers** are people who ___.
   a. are old
   b. have just come somewhere
   c. like new things

4. What word do you see inside **mountainous**? That word helps you guess that **mountainous** means ___.
   a. having many mountains
   b. having many fountains
   c. being very flat

5. What word do you see inside **cleanliness**? That word helps you guess that **cleanliness** means ___.
   a. being ugly
   b. being dirty
   c. being clean

6. What word do you see inside **shortage**? That word helps you guess that **shortage** means a number that is ___.
   a. too much
   b. not enough
   c. just right

7. What word do you see inside **livelihood**? That word helps you guess that **livelihood** means a way of ___.
   a. driving a car
   b. making money to live
   c. building a house

8. What words do you see inside **overnight**? Those words help you guess that **overnight** means ___.
   a. hard
   b. nice
   c. quickly

B. Write a sentence to answer each question below. Use the lesson word in dark type in your sentence.

1. How many class members are **newcomers** to your town this year?
2. What is the name of a famous U.S. **skyscraper**?
3. How did your grandfather earn his **livelihood**?

LESSON 2

Here are the eight new words in this lesson. Their meanings are not listed. Notice how the words are used in the story below. Look for a word you know in each new word. The words inside will help you guess the meanings of the new words.

especially	**addition**
national	**superior**
competition	**partially**
overcame	**underneath**

The Best

Kathy Arendsen is a winner. Kathy is the best softball pitcher in the U.S. She is **especially** good. She can throw a softball faster than almost anyone who ever played the game.

Kathy plays for the Hi-Ho Brakettes of Stratford, Connecticut. The Brakettes have been **national** champions for many years. They played against very good **competition** in order to be the champs. Year after year, they **overcame** the best women's teams from all over the country. In 1985, the Brakettes also won the world's softball championship.

One year Kathy pitched in 23 games and won all 23. In **addition** to a perfect record, Kathy is famous for her no-hitters. She has pitched 14 no-hitters in one season and continues to have a **superior** record.

Kathy is only **partially** the reason the Brakettes are so good. Another pitcher on the team, Barbara Reinalda, has helped make the team outstanding.

Kathy's best pitch is her fastball. It can go as fast as 96 miles per hour. Most batters don't have time to swing before the ball is past them for a strike. Her pitches also rise or fall as they come towards the batters. That makes many hitters swing above or **underneath** the pitches.

With Kathy pitching for them, the Brakettes are not just good, they are the best.

146

A. Look for words you know in the new words in Lesson 2. The words inside will help you pick the best meanings in the questions below. Put your answers on your paper.

1. What word do you see inside **especially**? That word helps you guess that **especially** means __.
   a. very or in a special way
   b. in an ordinary way
   c. in a new way

2. What word do you see inside **national**? That word helps you guess that **national** means belonging to __.
   a. a whole country
   b. a whole city
   c. a whole state

3. What word do you see almost spelled out in **competition**? That word helps you guess that **competition** means __.
   a. dogs and cats
   b. opponents or other teams
   c. complete

4. What words do you see inside **overcame**? Those words help you guess that **overcame** means __.
   a. did too much
   b. came to visit
   c. won over or beat

5. What word do you see inside **addition**? That word helps you guess that **addition** means __.
   a. something put in a dish
   b. something added
   c. arithmetic

6. What word do you see inside **superior**? That word helps you guess that **superior** means __.
   a. very good
   b. able to fly
   c. not very good

7. What word do you see inside **partially**? That word helps you guess that **partially** means __.
   a. totally
   b. sadly
   c. partly

8. What word do you see inside **underneath**? That word helps you guess that **underneath** means __.
   a. above
   b. below
   c. in the middle

B. Write a sentence to answer each question below. Use the lesson word in dark type in your sentence.

1. Which teacher that you had in the past was **especially** good?
2. Why do some people hide money **underneath** their mattresses?
3. Which was a **superior** team in baseball last year?

Choose the word or phrase that best completes each sentence. Put your answers on your answer sheet.

Test Tips: This kind of question asks you to think about the meaning of the key word. Then you need to use the meaning to choose the best answer. Read the sentence beginnings carefully. Use word parts to help you guess the meanings of the key words.

1. A superior runner usually finishes in __.
   a. first place
   b. last place
   c. the middle
   d. near the end

2. If there is a shortage of jobs, there are __.
   a. too many jobs
   b. not enough jobs
   c. not many tall people
   d. not enough money

3. To earn a livelihood, a person needs to get __.
   a. a house
   b. a car
   c. a friend
   d. a job

4. If you are partially sure of an answer, you are __.
   a. totally sure
   b. not totally sure
   c. not sure at all
   d. totally wrong

5. A solution that is found overnight is a __.
   a. slow one
   b. dark one
   c. quick one
   d. wrong one

6. Someone who overcame a sickness __.
   a. got worse
   b. got better
   c. is still sick
   d. has not been sick

148

UNIT III
STUDY SKILLS

PART 1: *Visual Materials* 150

PART 2: *Reference Skills* 174

You can get facts in many different ways:

A. By reading a passage.

Puerto Rico is three times the size of the state of Rhode Island. But it is only about half the size of Hawaii.

B. By looking at maps which are drawings of parts of the earth.

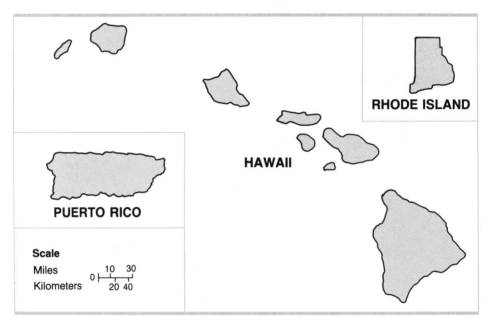

RHODE ISLAND

HAWAII

PUERTO RICO

Scale

Miles

Kilometers

0 10 30

20 40

C. By reading a table where facts are listed so that they can be read at a glance.

SIZES OF LAND	
Hawaii	6,425 square miles
Puerto Rico	3,435 square miles
Rhode Island	1,049 square miles

D. By looking at a graph where the facts really stand out.

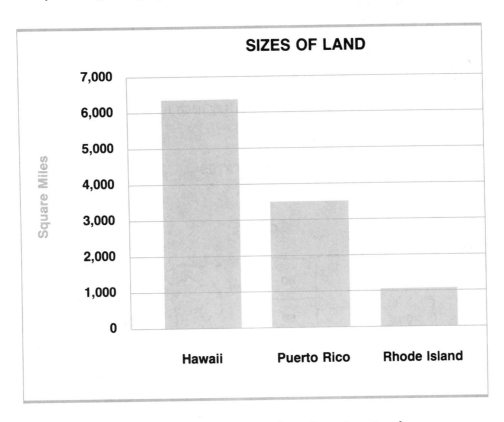

SIZES OF LAND

Read each question below. They are based on the visual materials you just studied. Be sure of your own answer before you study the choices. Write your answers on your paper.

1. Which shows how many islands there are in Hawaii?
   a. map
   b. table
   c. graph

2. Which one tells the exact size of Rhode Island?
   a. map
   b. table
   c. graph

Learn to read different kinds of visual materials in the following ten lessons. This skill can save you much time and work in getting facts.

LESSON 1

Where Presidents Come From

Does a person from Ohio or Virginia have a better chance of living in the White House than anyone else? It seems that way. Eight out of 40 U.S. Presidents came from Ohio. Eight came from Virginia. William Henry Harrison, the ninth U.S. President, had the best chance of all. Why? He was born in Virginia and then lived in Ohio.

Here is a map of the United States. You will see that Virginia and Ohio are not too far away from each other. New York, Massachusetts, and California are worth noting, too. They each have sent at least three of their native sons to the White House.

UNITED STATES

Maps are flat drawings of Earth or parts of it. The map on the left shows the shapes and sizes of the 50 states. Like most U.S. maps, it abbreviates the names of the states. Use the map to answer the questions below.

Choose the best answer.

1. President Lyndon Johnson came from the largest state on the Gulf of Mexico. He was from ___.
   a. Wyoming
   b. Montana
   c. Texas
   d. New Mexico

Check your answer. The state on the Gulf of Mexico with the largest land area has the abbreviation TX. The answer is **c.**

2. President Jimmy Carter is from Georgia. Which state is below Georgia on the map?
   a. Alabama
   b. South Carolina
   c. Tennessee
   d. Florida

3. President Harry Truman was from a state surrounded by Illinois and seven other states. He was from ___.
   a. Iowa
   b. Wisconsin
   c. Missouri
   d. Indiana

4. Which area of the United States has more states?
   a. near the Atlantic Ocean
   b. near the Pacific Ocean
   c. near Washington
   d. near the Gulf of Mexico

5. Which of these states is closest to Canada?
   a. Wyoming
   b. Oregon
   c. North Dakota
   d. South Dakota

Run, Terry, Run

Terry Fox had cancer. It left him with only one leg. Yet he became famous for running. He ran with an artificial leg to raise money to fight cancer. His plan was to run all the way across Canada, from St. John's to Vancouver. He would cross the water by boat. Terry started out in St. John's in April, 1981, and made it to the halfway point.

Terry had to give up the run at Thunder Bay when doctors found cancer in his lungs. He died on June 28, when he was 22 years old. He raised more money for the Canadian Cancer Society than he dreamed possible—over $24 million.

This map shows the route that Terry Fox planned to run and the part of the route he was able to cover.

CANADA

154

To follow Terry's run on a map, you must be able to find directions. The four main directions on a map are north, south, east, and west. Between the four main directions are four "halfway" directions. They are northeast (NE), northwest (NW), southeast (SE), southwest (SW). These directions appear on the map's compass rose. Find the compass rose at the bottom of the map.

Some maps use only an arrow pointing north. When you know which direction is north, you can figure out that south is below. West is to the left. East is to the right.

Choose the best answer.

1. Terry started his run in St. John's, on Canada's __ coast.
   a. north
   b. south
   c. east
   d. west

Check your answer. St. John's is on the right side of the map. The answer is **c**.

2. Terry planned to run from __.
   a. north to south
   b. east to west
   c. south to north
   d. west to east

3. Montreal is __ of St. John's.
   a. NE
   b. SE
   c. NW
   d. SW

4. The city that is west of Thunder Bay is __.
   a. St. John's
   b. Winnipeg
   c. Ottawa
   d. Montreal

5. From Winnipeg, the direction to Toronto is __.
   a. NE
   b. NW
   c. SE
   d. SW

Four Corners, U.S.A.

Gordon Yazzie is on his way home from Aneth, Utah. With long oars he takes the boat out on the brown-gray water of the San Juan River. He has started out in Utah. Then he follows the river to New Mexico. Soon he's almost home. He lives in Rattlesnake, New Mexico. Rattlesnake is part of the Navajo Indian Reservation.

The San Juan River flows almost across Four Corners. Four Corners is the only point in the U.S. where four states come together. The map below shows exactly where the corners of Utah, Colorado, Arizona, and New Mexico meet.

FOUR CORNERS

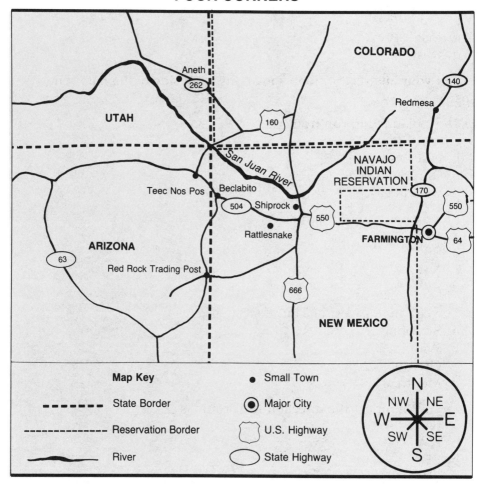

At the bottom of the map of Four Corners is a map key. The key shows the symbols used on the map. These symbols stand for features such as small towns, major cities, highways, rivers, and borders. Use the map key and the map to answer the questions below.

Choose the best answer.

1. Aneth, Utah is northwest of Four Corners. Aneth is a __.
   a. small town
   b. river
   c. state highway
   d. major city

Check your answer. The symbol next to Aneth is ● . The answer is **a**.

2. Route 160 crosses Four Corners from Colorado to Arizona. This route is a __.
   a. state border
   b. state highway
   c. U.S. highway
   d. river

3. Which town is closest to Four Corners?
   a. Beclabito, New Mexico
   b. Aneth, Utah
   c. Redmesa, Colorado
   d. Teec Nos Pos, Arizona

4. What is the name of the biggest city near Four Corners?
   a. Farmington
   b. Shiprock
   c. Rattlesnake
   d. Red Rock Trading Post

5. Suppose Gordon Yazzie drives from his home in Rattlesnake to Farmington. Which U.S. highway should he use?
   a. 160
   b. 550
   c. 504
   d. 666

Meet Stevie Wonder

Up close, Stevie Wonder doesn't act like someone who is totally blind. "I never knew what it was like to see. So being blind is no different from seeing," Stevie says. Like any person who can see, he goes to the movies and watches TV. (Friends tell him what's happening on the screen.) He turns the lights on and off when he goes into the bathroom. He has even flown a plane.

Stevie opens the first show in the November Rock concerts on Tuesday. Look at the November calendar below to find out when Stevie and other rock stars will appear.

NOVEMBER ROCK 1986

SUN.	MON.	TUES.	WED.	THURS.	FRI.	SAT.
		1 STEVIE WONDER 2 Shows Nightly: 8:00, 10:00	2	3	4	5 Tonight Only TEARS FOR FEARS All Tickets $10.00
6	7	8	9	10	11	12
13	14	15	16	17	18	19 BRUCE SPRING-STEEN 8:00, 10:00 $8.00
20	21	22	23	24 Special Holiday Treat TINA TURNER 9:30, 11:00 Tickets: $6, $8, $10	25	26
27 Today at Noon DIANA ROSS (sold out)	28	29	30			

A calendar is a kind of table because the dates and days of the week are arranged in columns and rows. A column goes up and down. A row goes from side to side. All the dates in one column fall on the same day of the week. All the dates in one row appear in the same week.

Use the November Rock calendar to answer the questions below.

Choose the best answer.

1. On which day of every week is there no show?
   a. Sunday
   b. Monday
   c. Thursday
   d. Friday

Check your answer. The column under MON. has no shows listed. The answer is **b**.

2. On what date is the Diana Ross Sunday show?
   a. the 6th
   b. the 13th
   c. the 20th
   d. the 27th

3. If you want to go to a Saturday night show, whom can you see?
   a. Bruce Springsteen or Diana Ross
   b. Tears for Fears or Stevie Wonder
   c. Tears for Fears or Bruce Springsteen
   d. Bruce Springsteen or Tina Turner

4. Thanksgiving Day is always on the fourth Thursday of November. Which show can you see on Thanksgiving Day?
   a. Tina Turner
   b. Bruce Springsteen
   c. Tears for Fears
   d. Diana Ross

5. Which week has the most shows?
   a. Nov. 6 to 12
   b. Nov. 13 to 19
   c. Nov. 20 to 26
   d. Nov. 27 to Dec. 3

The Train Ride—146 Years Later!

The year was 1839. Vice President Richard M. Johnson was in New York City on his way to Philadelphia. He was expected at a meeting at 6:30 that evening. When did he begin his trip? At noon! In 1839, it took six and one-half hours by train and ferry to get from New York City to Philadelphia. That wasn't so bad. In 1817, the trip took three days!

If this were a cold winter day, Vice President Johnson would have started much earlier. The Delaware River might freeze over. There would be no ferry and he would have had to walk across the ice.

Today, it's possible to leave New York City on the 9:00 a.m. train and be in Philadelphia at 10:29 a.m. In fact, some people live in New York City and work in Philadelphia. They use the train schedule below.

NY · NJ · PA TRAIN SCHEDULE						
Train Number	61 a.m.	89 a.m.	181 a.m.	141 a.m.	211 a.m.	169 p.m.
New York, NY	7:00	8:00	9:00	10:00	11:00	**12:00**
Newark, NJ	7:15	8:13	9:12	10:12	11:13	**12:12**
Metro Park, NJ	7:31	8:28	—	—	—	—
New Brunswick, NJ	—	8:38	—	10:32	11:33	—
Princeton, NJ	—	—	9:44	—	11:48	—
Trenton, NJ	8:03	8:58	9:56	10:55	11:58	**12:52**
Philadelphia, PA	8:36	9:36	10:29	11:28	**12:32**	**1:23**

How do you read the train schedule? Suppose you're in New York City and you want to go to Princeton. Run your finger down the list of cities to find Princeton. Next, move your finger to the right. You will see the times that trains arrive in Princeton. Then run your finger up to the times listed across from New York. That's when the trains leave New York. Make your choice and enjoy the ride!

Choose the best answer.

1. A doctor's office in Philadelphia opens at 9:00 a.m. What time must the doctor leave New York City to get there on time?

   a. 7:00 a.m.
   b. 8:00 a.m.
   c. 9:00 a.m.
   d. 10:00 a.m.

Check your answer. The train that arrives in Philadelphia at 8:36 a.m. is in the second column, right next to the listing of places. The time listed right next to New York is 7:00 a.m. The answer is **a**.

2. Suppose Vice President Johnson rode today's trains. What time would he have to leave New York to be in Philadelphia by 1:30 p.m.?
   a. 9:00 a.m.
   b. 10:00 a.m.
   c. 11:00 a.m.
   d. 12:00 noon

3. You board the train in Newark at 8:13. When do you arrive in Trenton?
   a. 8:03 a.m.
   b. 8:58 a.m.
   c. 9:56 a.m.
   d. 10:55 a.m.

4. Which is the fastest train to Philadelphia?
   a. 69
   b. 89
   c. 211
   d. 169

5. Which two trains make the most stops?
   a. 61 and 89   c. 89 and 211
   b. 181 and 169   d. 181 and 141

Belize Is Born

The world has been changing a lot. Since 1975, more than a dozen new nations have appeared. One of the newest is Belize, a tiny nation near Mexico. The British had ruled Belize for 300 years. But by 1981, the people of Belize were ready to rule themselves. One day in September the British flag came down. The red, white, and blue flag of Belize went up. Belize was independent at last.

Find out more about new nations by looking at the table below. Each of these nations was once ruled by another nation.

Six New Nations 1975-1985			
Nation	Number of People	Languages Spoken	Date of Independence
Angola	7,770,000	Portuguese, Bantu	Nov. 11, 1975
Belize	154,000	English, Spanish	Sept. 21, 1981
Djibouti	316,000	Somali, French	June 27, 1977
Mozambique	13,047,000	Portuguese	June 25, 1975
Tuvalu	8,000	Tuvaluan, English	Oct. 1, 1978
Vanuatu	130,000	Bislamu, French	July 30, 1980

A table is arranged in columns and rows. A column goes up and down. Each column has a title. The title tells what kinds of facts are in the column. For example, all the words in the first column are nations.

A row in a table goes across, from side to side. Each row has facts about the nation in the first column. For example, one fact about Angola is that it has 7,700,000 people.

Use the table about new nations to answer the questions below.

Choose the best answer.

1. Which nation on the table has over ten million people?
   a. Angola
   b. Djibouti
   c. Mozambique
   d. Tuvalu

Check your answer. Look down the column that shows the number of people. Find the number that is almost ten million and find the nation in the same row. The answer is **c**.

2. Which nation was the last to become independent?
   a. Tuvalu
   b. Belize
   c. Djibouti
   d. Mozambique

3. Which nation has the fewest people?
   a. Belize
   b. Angola
   c. Vanuatu
   d. Tuvalu

4. Which two nations became independent within five months of the same year?
   a. Angola and Tuvalu
   b. Angola and Vanuatu
   c. Tuvalu and Belize
   d. Mozambique and Angola

5. Which two nations were probably ruled by English-speaking people?
   a. Belize and Tuvalu
   b. Djibouti and Vanuatu
   c. Angola and Mozambique
   d. Djibouti and Angola

How Much Time for TV?

Once upon a time, there was no television. That wasn't because no one had tried to invent it. Scientists had worked on the idea starting in the late 1800's. Many years passed before television worked well.

In the 1940's, television caught on. It was a hit from the beginning. Soon the movie business, the restaurant business, and even the jukebox business went down. Americans stayed home to watch television. How much watching do people do? The graph below can help you decide.

This graph is called a pictograph. It shows the average number of hours a day that people have watched television in different years.

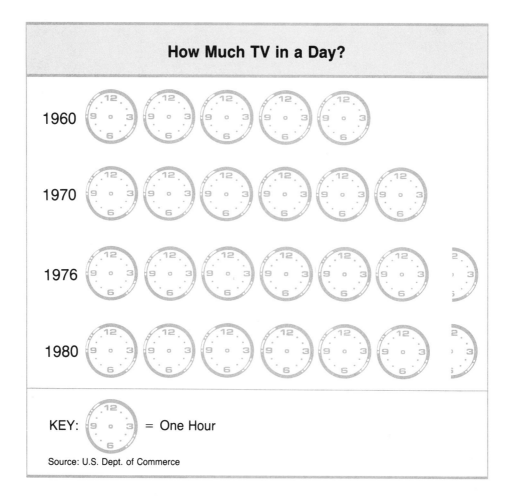

A pictograph uses pictures, or symbols, to show information. In the graph at the left, the symbol is a clock. Find the key at the bottom. The key tells you that each clock on the graph equals one hour of television watching. Half a clock equals one-half hour of watching.

To read the graph, count the number of clocks in the row for each year. A row runs across, from side to side. Use the graph to answer the questions below.

Choose the best answer.

1. The average number of hours spent watching TV in 1960 was ___.
    a. 5 hours
    b. 5½ hours
    c. 6 hours
    d. 6½ hours

Check your answer. There are five clocks in the row beside 1960. The answer is **a**.

2. People spent an average of six hours a day watching TV in ___.
    a. 1960
    b. 1970
    c. 1976
    d. 1980

3. From 1970 to 1976, television watching ___.
    a. didn't change
    b. went up by one-half hour
    c. went up by one hour
    d. went down by one-half hour

4. Television watching went up the most from ___.
    a. 1960 to 1970
    b. 1970 to 1976
    c. 1970 to 1980
    d. 1976 to 1980

5. In which two years did the number of hours stay the same?
    a. 1960 and 1970
    b. 1970 and 1976
    c. 1970 and 1980
    d. 1976 and 1980

The Slowest and the Fastest

The state of Florida was once almost gobbled up by snails. They were giant snails from Africa. A visitor took some to Florida, where they spread quickly. Some of the snails were as big as a person's hand. They ate the leaves on trees and other plants. They had to be stopped, and they were. Poison killed thousands of the snails, and Florida was saved.

Catching a snail should be easier than catching any other animal. The snail is the slowest of all land animals. Its top speed is 55 yards per hour. At this speed it would take the snail about 32 hours to travel one mile. A snail only goes that fast when it's very hungry.

The bar graph below shows some other top speeds.

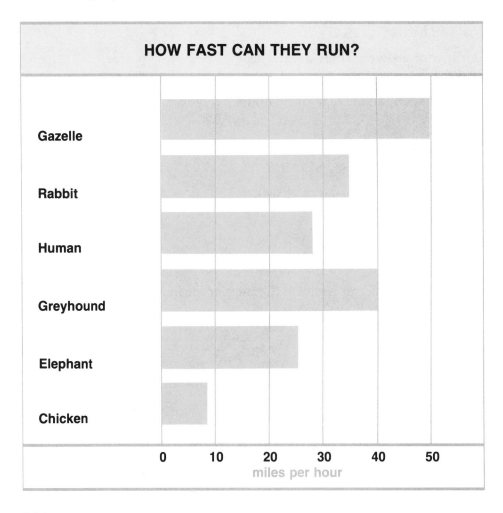

166

A bar graph has bars of different lengths, instead of pictures. This kind of graph makes it easy to compare several things quickly. To read the graph, notice where each bar ends. Then find the closest number at the bottom of the graph.

Use the bar graph about running speeds to answer the questions.

Choose the best answer.

1. What is the top speed of a rabbit?
   a. 30 miles per hour
   b. 35 miles per hour
   c. 40 miles per hour
   d. 50 miles per hour

Check your answer. The bar for the rabbit is halfway between 30 and 40, or 35. The answer is **b**.

2. Fifty miles per hour is the top speed for ___.
   a. a rabbit
   b. a human
   c. a greyhound
   d. a gazelle

3. What is the difference in running speed between a greyhound and a gazelle?
   a. 5 miles per hour
   b. 10 miles per hour
   c. 15 miles per hour
   d. 20 miles per hour

4. The closest to an elephant in running speed is ___.
   a. a human
   b. a greyhound
   c. a chicken
   d. a rabbit

5. A rabbit and greyhound can both run faster than ___.
   a. 50 miles per hour
   b. 45 miles per hour
   c. 40 miles per hour
   d. 30 miles per hour

The Tin Lizzie

It shook, rattled, and groaned. It wasn't pretty. It looked like a black box sitting on high, skinny wheels. But it could go anywhere, and it was cheap.

What was it? It was Henry Ford's Model-T car—better known as the Tin Lizzie. This car was the most popular of all for nearly 20 years. It changed the American way of life forever.

Model T's were sold as fast as they were made. Eleven thousand were sold in 1908. They cost $850 each. Of course, you can't buy a new car for $850 any longer. The prices of new cars keep changing.

The line graph below shows how the average prices of American cars have been changing.

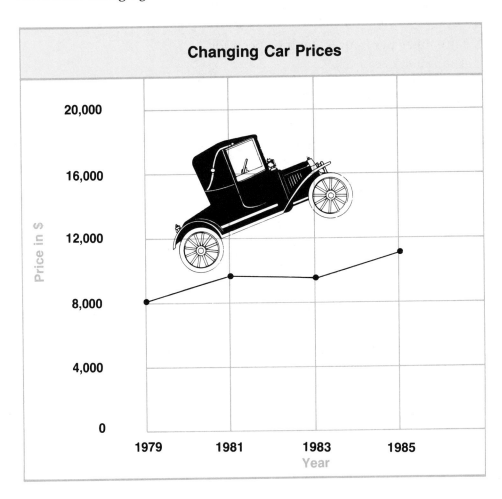

A line graph shows how something has changed. This kind of graph uses a simple line to show changes. If the line goes up, that means things have gone up in some way. If the line goes down, then something has gone down.

Suppose you want to find the average price of cars for 1979. Find 1979 at the bottom of the graph. Find the dot over the year. Then find the price across from the dot.

Use the line graph to answer the questions below.

Choose the best answer.

1. What was the average price of a car in 1979?
   a. $4,000
   b. $6,000
   c. $8,000
   d. $10,000

Check your answer. The dot above 1979 is across from the number 8,000. The answer is **c**.

2. What does the line graph show about car prices?
   a. They have been going up.
   b. They have been going down.
   c. They have not changed.
   d. They have been cut in half.

3. In what year did cars cost more than $7,000 but less than $9,000?
   a. 1979
   b. 1981
   c. 1983
   d. 1985

4. Suppose you were looking for a new car in 1981. What would the average price have been?
   a. less than $6,000
   b. less than $8,000
   c. more than $8,000
   d. more than $10,000

5. How did the average price of cars change from 1983 to 1985?
   a. It went up by about $500.
   b. It went up by about $1,500.
   c. It went down by about $500.
   d. It went down by about $1,500.

The New Americans

Rita and Maria Rivera are sisters. They used to live in Cuba. They left Cuba on a crowded boat to come to the United States. Tom Nguyen also left his country, Vietnam, to come to the United States. Rita, Maria, and Tom are American immigrants. They have made new homes in their new land. More than 400,000 immigrants enter the U.S. in a year. Most come to find more freedom and a better life for the future.

Where do most of the immigrants come from? Look at the pie graph below. Notice which parts of the world are the bigger pieces of the pie. Cuba is in Latin America. Vietnam is in Asia.

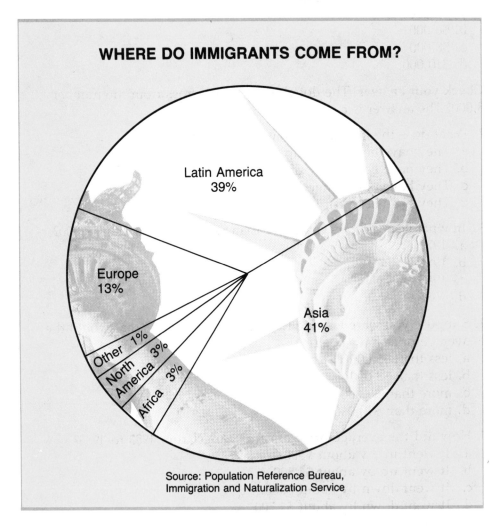

WHERE DO IMMIGRANTS COME FROM?

Latin America 39%

Europe 13%

Asia 41%

Other 1%

North America 3%

Africa 3%

Source: Population Reference Bureau, Immigration and Naturalization Service

You can divide a pie into pieces. That's also the idea of a pie graph, or circle graph. A pie graph shows how the whole amount of something is divided into parts.

The pie graph at the left has a number in each part. These numbers are percentages, or parts of 100 percent. All the numbers add up to 100%—all the immigrants who come to the U.S. Use the graph to answer the questions below.

Choose the best answer.

1. The graph shows that most immigrants to the U.S. come from __.
   a. Latin America
   b. Asia
   c. Europe
   d. North America

Check your answer. The biggest part of the circle is Asia. The answer is **b**.

2. Africa has only a small part of the circle because __.
   a. none of the immigrants come from there
   b. few of the immigrants come from there
   c. many of the immigrants come from there
   d. all of the immigrants come from there

3. More immigrants come to the U.S. from Europe than from __.
   a. Africa
   b. Latin America
   c. Asia
   d. the rest of the world

4. About the same number of immigrants come from __.
   a. Europe and North America
   b. Europe and Asia
   c. Africa and North America
   d. North America and Latin America

5. What percent of all immigrants are from Latin America and Asia?
   a. 39%
   b. 41%
   c. 50%
   d. 80%

TAKING TESTS

Sometimes, tests include exercises based on visual materials such as maps, tables, and graphs. Follow the test tips on the next two pages. Put your answers on your answer sheet.

Test Tips: Know which visual material would be most useful in getting a certain kind of information.

Choose the best answer.

1. Which would show you the date of the first Monday in May?
   a. map   c. calendar
   b. circle graph d. pictograph

2. Which one of these would best show how the price of blue jeans has gone up since 1980?
   a. circle graph c. table
   b. line graph   d. map

3. Which one of these would best show how many people live in Florida, Texas, and California?
   a. map   c. table
   b. circle graph d. pictograph

4. Which one of these would you use to find out which roads go from Newark to Jacksonville?
   a. map   c. table
   b. calendar   d. graph

Test Tips: On a map-reading test, the first thing to do is to study the map quickly. Look at the key. Know where north, south, east, and west are. Then read each question. Look at the map again to find the answer.

5. What direction would you travel in going from Linton to Hazleton?
   a. north   c. east
   b. south   d. west

6. Which town is west of Bismarck?
   a. Sterling Steele c. Mandan
   b. Long Lake   d. Linton

7. What route from the west joins Route 6 south of Bismarck?
   a. 83   c. 3
   b. 21   d. 13

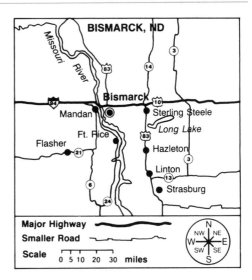

172

Test Tips: Some test questions are based on a kind of graph. First, have a quick look at each graph. Then read each question. Be sure of your own answer before you check it against the graph.

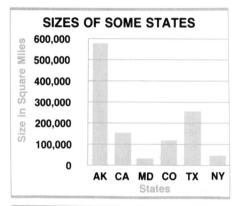

SIZES OF SOME STATES

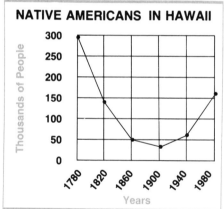

NATIVE AMERICANS IN HAWAII

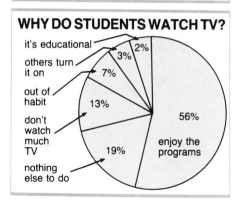

WHY DO STUDENTS WATCH TV?

Choose the best answer.

1. Which is the largest state?
   a. MD   c. TX
   b. NY   d. AK

2. Which state is smaller than Colorado but larger than Maryland?
   a. NY   c. CO
   b. TX   d. MD

3. In what period was there the greatest drop in the number of Native Americans in Hawaii?
   a. 1780–1820   c. 1900–1940
   b. 1860–1900   d. 1940–1980

4. In what period was there an increase in the number of Native Americans in Hawaii?
   a. 1780–1900   c. 1820–1900
   b. 1900–1980   d. 1780–1820

5. For every 100 students, how many watch TV because there is nothing else to do?
   a. 56   c. 7
   b. 13   d. 19

6. Which is the most popular reason for watching TV?
   a. out of habit
   b. it's educational
   c. enjoy the programs
   d. others turn it on

PART 2 *Reference Skills*

Suppose you are looking for facts about your favorite sport. How did the sport begin? What special words are used in it? Which players hold the best records? These are only some of the interesting facts you can find.

What reference materials will give the facts you need? There are many different kinds of sources. Here are some of them.

A. Dictionary

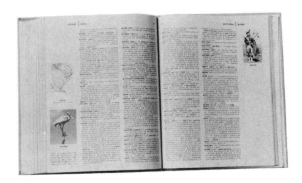

C. Encyclopedia

B. Almanac

D. Books

E. Newspapers and Magazines

Must you read all these references to find the new facts you need? No! Just know where to look. Do you know which one to use for what you need? Test yourself. Read each question below. Choose the best answer. Write your answers on your paper.

1. Which one would you use to find the meaning of a word?
  a. dictionary
  b. almanac
  c. encyclopedia
  d. magazine

2. Which one would you use to find the score of yesterday's game?
  a. almanac
  b. a sports book
  c. encyclopedia
  d. newspaper

How do you find facts in each of these references? The following lessons will show you.

This Man's Number One

Millions of people have their names listed in the Manhattan telephone book in New York. Alec Aaarman is special, however. His name came first in the book in 1981. The year before the telephone company did not spell his name right. They spelled it Aarman. So John Aab was the first name listed in the telephone book.

Alec loves being first. Everyone can't be first like Alec. Someone has to be last. In 1981, the last person listed in the telephone book was N. Zzherobrouskievskieskieea.

People are listed in the telephone book by their last names. The names are arranged in the order of the alphabet, from A to Z. When two names begin with the same letter, the second letter is used in deciding the alphabetical order. When two last names are spelled the same, the first names are alphabetized.

Look at the names in the list below. Are they in alphabetical order?

Hickel — Hilton

Hickel, Jos.   22 S. 18th St. **555-6747**

Hickel, W.   195 Rorer Rd. **555-5921**

Higgins, Arthur   25 Myrtle Ave. **555-5291**

Hill, Gloria   292 N. Wood St. **555-2120**

Hill, H.D.   622 Pine Blvd. **555-3026**

Hill, Harry   32 S. 9th St. **555-2904**

Hill, Hattie   6409 Bath Pl. **555-1105**

Hillo, Saml.   41 Thayer Ave. **555-1015**

Hill's Market   251 Pine Blvd. **555-3206**

Choose the best answer.

1. The name John Hiedel will appear between ___.
   a. Hickel, Jos. and Hickel, W.
   b. Hickel, W. and Higgins, Arthur
   c. Hill, Gloria and Hill, H.D.
   d. no names in the list

Check your answer. The last name is used to decide the order. The first two letters in *Hiedel* are the same as in the other names. Use the third letter in finding the alphabetical order. The answer is **b**.

2. Hill's Top is the name of a store. It may appear in the telephone listing ___.
   a. between Hill, Gloria and Hill's Market
   b. between Hillo, Saml. and Hill's Market
   c. before Hill's Market
   d. after all the names

3. Which of the following words will appear first in the order of the alphabet?
   a. corn
   b. copy
   c. crab
   d. chair

4. Which of the following words will appear last in the alphabetical order?
   a. until
   b. unlucky
   c. unfortunate
   d. unhappy

5. Where would your name be in a telephone book?
   a. before David Anderson
   b. between David Anderson and Ellen Ash
   c. between Lou Burns and Jane Diaz
   d. after Jane Diaz

How a Word Was Born From an Elephant

The word *jumbo* did not become a word until 1882. It was a name given to a circus elephant. Jumbo was the largest elephant then. What can *jumbo* mean today?

One sure way of finding the meaning of a word is to look it up in the dictionary. Do you want to find the word quickly? Use the guide words. These are two words that appear at the top of each page in the dictionary. The guide word on the left is the first word whose meaning is given on the page. The guide word on the right is the last word defined on the page. Other words come in alphabetical order between the two guide words.

Here's a page from a dictionary. Find *jumbo*.

juggler

jug·gler (jŭg´lər) person who performs the trick of keeping objects moving rapidly in the air.

jug·u·lar (jŭg´yə lər) having to do with the neck or throat; especially naming either of the large veins, the **jugular veins,** on either side of the neck.

juice (jōōs) liquid part of vegetables, fruits, meats, etc.: *tomato* juice; *apple* juice.

juic·y (jōō´sĭ) full of juice: *a juicy orange.* **juic·i·er, juic·i·est; juic·i·ly.**

Ju·ly (jōō lī´) seventh month of the year. July has 31 days.

jum·ble (jŭm´bəl) **1** to mix in a confused way; put together without order: *He jumbled the letters of the word and asked us to guess what they spelled.* **2** confused mass; disorder: *Books and papers were in a jumble on the desk.* **jum·bled, jum·bling.**

jum·bo (jŭm´bō) **1** large; huge: *a jumbo ice-cream cone.* **2** large, clumsy person, animal, or thing. **jum·bos.**

jump (jŭmp) **1** a leap, spring, or bound: *a high jump off a diving board.* **2** to leap, spring, or bound: *to jump over a puddle.* **3** to cause (something) to leap, spring, or bound: *to jump a horse over a hurdle.* **4** sudden start: *The baby gave a startled jump at the loud noise.* **5** to give a sudden start: *Helen jumped in fright at the strange sound.* **6** sudden rise: *a jump in temperature.* **7** to rise suddenly: *The price of wheat just jumped three cents on the bushel.* **8** to pass or move abruptly (from one thing to another): *The conversation jumped from one subject to another.*

juror

June (jōōn) sixth month of the year. June has 30 days.

jun·gle (jŭng´gəl) land covered with a thick growth of plants, trees, and vines.

jun·ior (jōōn´yər) **1** person who is younger (than another): *He is my junior by six years.* **2** of lower standing or position: *the junior partner in a business.* **3** of or having to do with the third year of a four-year course in high school or college: *The junior dance will be held in May.* **4** member of this class: *Fred is a junior in college.* **5** Junior the younger (used to describe a son named for his father): *James Stone, Junior.*

¹**junk** (jŭngk) **1** useless articles; trash: *Let's throw away that old junk in the attic.* **2** to discard (a thing) as worthless or useless: *We finally junked our old car.* [¹**junk** is from an Old French word (jonc) meaning ''a plant with a hollow stem,'' ''a string,'' ''a cord,'' which goes back to a Latin word (juncus) meaning ''a reed.'' ¹**junk** used to mean ''cord,'' then ''old or discarded cord,'' and finally anything old or ready to be thrown away.]

²**junk** (jŭngk) kind of Chinese sailing vessel with a flat bottom and high stern. [²**junk** comes through Portuguese (junco) from the word of a South Pacific language (jong).]

Chinese junk

ju·ror (jōōr´ər) member of a jury.

Choose the best answer.

1. The word *jumbo* appears between the guide words *juggler* and ___.
   a. jump
   b. junction
   c. juror
   d. juncture

   Check your answer. *Jumbo* comes after the word *jumble* and before *jump*.
   The guide words are *juggler* and *juror*. The answer is **c**.

2. On the same dictionary page, you will find *junior* closer to the guide
   word ___.
   a. juggler
   b. juncture
   c. jungle
   d. juror

3. In one dictionary, the word *skill* would appear on the page with the
   guide words ___.
   a. sith and skate
   b. skateboard and skiff
   c. skiffle and skirmish
   d. skirr and slack

4. Look at the words below. Which will not appear on the page with the
   guide words *zero* and *zodiac*?
   a. zigzag
   b. zoo
   c. zip
   d. zero hour

5. You will find *library* between ___.
   a. letter and level
   b. lever and libel
   c. libel and licit
   d. life and light

Borrowed Words

How often do you hear people say, "Let's barbecue hamburgers on the patio"? The words *barbecue* and *patio* are from Spanish. *Hamburger* is from German. As people from different parts of the world come to live in America, they bring their own language with them. Some of their words soon become part of the American English language. These words then become entries in the dictionary of American English. Below is a dictionary entry.

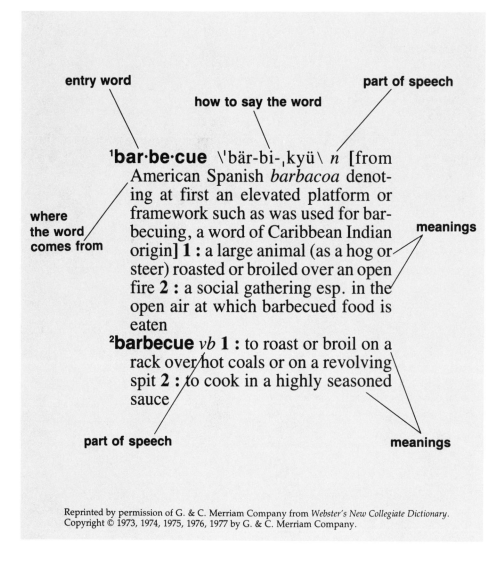

entry word

how to say the word

part of speech

where the word comes from

meanings

¹**bar·be·cue** \'bär-bi-ˌkyü\ *n* [from American Spanish *barbacoa* denoting at first an elevated platform or framework such as was used for barbecuing, a word of Caribbean Indian origin] **1** : a large animal (as a hog or steer) roasted or broiled over an open fire **2** : a social gathering esp. in the open air at which barbecued food is eaten

²**barbecue** *vb* **1** : to roast or broil on a rack over hot coals or on a revolving spit **2** : to cook in a highly seasoned sauce

part of speech

meanings

Look at the dictionary entry on page 180. The first thing you see on the left is the entry word in dark type, divided into syllables. Next, you see symbols, telling you how to say the word. Then the dictionary tells you whether the word is a noun *(n)* or a verb *(vb)*. If the word is borrowed, the dictionary will say where it came from. Finally, you see the meaning of the word. If the word has more than one meaning, each meaning has a number.

Choose the best answer.

1. How many syllables are in the word *barbecue*?
   a. 2
   b. 3
   c. 4
   d. 5

Check Your Answer. The entry word in dark type is divided into three parts. The answer is **b**.

2. The last syllable of *barbecue* rhymes with which word?
   a. few \'fyü\
   b. cup \'kəp\
   c. buy \'bī\
   d. tub \'təb\

3. How many meanings does the noun *barbecue* have?
   a. one
   b. two
   c. three
   d. four

4. The verb *barbecue* means __.
   a. a large animal
   b. a hot sauce
   c. to roast over hot coals
   d. a social gathering

5. Which meaning of the word *barbecue* is used in this sentence: "Please come to the barbecue next Sunday"?
   a. a roasted animal
   b. a social gathering
   c. to roast over hot coals
   d. to cook in a hot sauce

Very Strange People

A man falls out of his plane and falls back into it again. Two people row a small boat from New York to England in 56 days. One person is so big, he wouldn't fit in any hospital room. Would you believe these stories? Well, they may sound strange but they did happen. James Cornell has more strange but true stories like these in a book called *Very Strange People*.

Here is part of the table of contents of *Very Strange People*. The table of contents lists the names of the chapters or parts of the book. It also tells on what page each chapter begins.

Very Strange People

Chapter		Page
One	A Dog's Life	3
Two	A Born-Again Pilot	14
Three	High Wire Act	33
Four	Fat Folks	41
Five	Over the Falls	43
Six	The Unending House	53
Seven	Row, Row, Row Your Boat	60
Eight	The Tower Builder	85

Unlike many reference materials, the table of contents is not arranged alphabetically. The chapters are listed in the order that they appear in the book.

Choose the best answer.

1. In 1918, Captain Hedley fell out of his plane in midair. Then he fell back into it again! You would most likely read about this pilot in Chapter __.
   a. 2   c. 5
   b. 3   d. 6

Check your answer. Someone who flies a plane is called a pilot. The pilot, Captain Hedley, could have lost his life. He didn't. The answer is **a**.

2. One morning in New York City, people saw a man walking on a tightrope between two tall buildings. You would most likely read this story in Chapter __.
   a. 1   c. 5
   b. 3   d. 8

3. The Earl of Bridgewater fed his dogs better than most people feed their friends. This story probably begins on page __.
   a. 3   c. 41
   b. 33   d. 85

4. Sarah Winchester thought she would die as soon as her house was finished. So she kept on adding more and more rooms. Her story most likely appears on page __.
   a. 43   c. 60
   b. 53   d. 85

5. Because of his great size, Robert Hughes could not enter any hospital room. This story appears before which story?
   a. A Born-Again Pilot   c. Fat Folks
   b. High Wire Act   d. Over the Falls

The Chinese, People of the Central Country

The people in China don't call themselves "Chinese." You will never hear them call their own country "China." The Chinese word for their country means "Central Country." Of course, they want to be called "people of the Central Country."

These facts come from the book called *China* by Daniel Chu. What else does the book talk about? The index in the back pages of the book will tell you. A part of the book's index is shown below.

Index

arts, 64–70, 126–131*
daily life, 76–109, 173–182
economy, 120–125*, 173–182,
   216–217
families, 79–85, 81*, 85*
farming, 88–93, 90*, 92*
food, 10–12, 68–70, 69*
geography, 15–20, 112*, 115*
holidays and festivals, 93–96
language, 49–54, 222–223
maps, 6, 11, 19, 30–31, 73, 137,
   157, 165
names, 77–78
people, 21–24, 23*, 116–119*
population, 10, 21, 136–137, 229
poverty, 10
religion, 35–46
size, 16

* Photograph

Use the index from the book *China* to answer these questions.

Choose the best answer.

1. Which of these pages might describe the daily life of the "people of the Central Country"?
   a. 10
   b. 21–24
   c. 76–109
   d. 93–96

Check your answer. The pages that tell about the people are on 21–24. But the key word in the question is *life*. So, the answer is **c**.

2. If you want to know how big the "Central Country" is, on what page will you start to read?
   a. 10
   b. 15
   c. 16
   d. 88

3. Which of these words give the pages that will have facts about the Chinese New Year?
   a. daily life
   b. holidays and festivals
   c. names
   d. religion

4. Which pages have photographs or pictures of farms?
   a. 64–70
   b. 90 and 92
   c. 30 and 31
   d. 116–119

5. The words in the index are in the order of the alphabet. Therefore, *families* comes before *farming* and right after ___.
   a. economy
   b. art
   c. people
   d. religion

Library Mystery

The case is about a missing book. You must find it among millions of other books in the library. But you have only one clue—the book's name or title. Is that enough to solve this case? It should be enough if you know how to use the card catalog.

The card catalog lists each book in the library on a card. The cards help you track down the book you want. The card catalog is a set of drawers filled with cards. On the front of each drawer is a printed label showing single letters (A – C; D – E) or groups of letters (Fa – Gru; Gry – He). These labels are called outside guides. If the first letters of the book's title, author, or subject fall within these outside guides, a card about the book might be in that drawer.

Here are three catalog cards on the same book.

AUTHOR CARD

```
364.12
F        Fast, Rodney T.
             My Business Card Says Private Eye

         Boston, Waterhouse Press © 1981
         136 p.

         Describes a private detective's most
         difficult cases.
```

TITLE CARD

```
364.12
F        My Business Card Says Private Eye
         Fast, Rodney T.

         Boston, Waterhouse Press © 1981
         136 p.

         Describes a private detective's most
         difficult cases.
```

```
364.12
F        PRIVATE DETECTIVES
         Fast, Rodney T.
             My Business Card Says Private Eye

         Boston, Waterhouse Press © 1981
         136 p.

         Describes a private detective's most
         difficult cases.
```

SUBJECT CARD

186

Look at the cards on page **186** to answer these questions.

Choose the best answer.

1. Suppose you know only the book's name. You would find the title card in the drawer labeled __.

  a. Bl–Ca

  b. Ma–Mn

  c. Mo–Mz

  d. Pr–Pu

Check your answer. Catalog cards are arranged in the order of the alphabet. What is the first word in the title? The answer is **c**.

2. Which drawer would have the author card for *My Business Card Says Private Eye?*

  a. Fa–Fo

  b. Pl–Pr

  c. Ra–Ro

  d. T–U

3. Rodney Fast's book is about __.

  a. unsolved cases

  b. business cards

  c. private detectives

  d. science

4. What kind of card would you look for to find other books by Rodney Fast?

  a. subject

  b. author

  c. title

  d. business

5. On which card would you find other books about crime?

  a. subject

  b. author

  c. title

  d. business

When Big Is Not Always Big

In Spanish, Rio Grande means *Big River*. The Rio Grande does not always live up to its name, however. There are times when you can cross the river without getting your ankles wet. But, in the spring, the rains come. The river bed fills up. Then the Rio Grande truly becomes the Big River that divides the United States and Mexico.

The Rio Grande starts in San Juan County, Colorado, and empties into the Gulf of Mexico at the other end. The river is more than 1,800 miles long.

How did the writer put together the little story about the "Big River"? The following reference books gave all the needed facts:

The Encyclopedia. It has important and very complete information on just about everything. It gives facts about people, places, and most anything that you would like to know. Just name it. Then look it up, like looking up a word in the dictionary. The subjects in an encyclopedia are alphabetized.

The Almanac. It has mostly up-to-date facts. (It also gives bits and pieces of information from the past.) This means that an almanac can tell you what went on in different parts of the world in the past year. A new almanac is printed each year.

188

Choose the best answer.

1. You want to know as many facts as you can about the Rio Grande. Which reference would you use?
   a. an encyclopedia
   b. an almanac
   c. a magazine
   d. a dictionary

   Check your answer. An encyclopedia has more facts about places than any of the other references. The answer is **a**.

2. Which reference will show the next day's weather for a town on the Rio Grande?
   a. an encyclopedia
   b. an almanac
   c. a newspaper
   d. a dictionary

3. Mexico lies south of the Rio Grande. How much oil does the United States buy from Mexico? How many people now live in Mexico City? You need the answers to those questions fast. Which of these books can help you?
   a. an encyclopedia
   b. an almanac
   c. a telephone book
   d. a dictionary

4. Where will you look to find the meaning of the word *reference*?
   a. in an encyclopedia
   b. in an almanac
   c. in a newspaper
   d. in a dictionary

5. Where can you find interesting facts about how nature, people, and time can change a river?
   a. in an encyclopedia
   b. in an almanac
   c. in a telephone book
   d. in a dictionary

Encyclopedia Riddles

Are you good at riddles? OK, where does Thomas Edison meet the Wolfman? Where do the Great Smoky Mountains meet Smoky the Bear? Give up? The answer is: an encyclopedia. An encyclopedia has articles on hundreds of subjects. The articles are in alphabetical order by topic. So, finding information never has to be a riddle. Use these encyclopedia volumes to help you answer the questions.

190

Choose the best answer.

1. Which volume would probably have an article that explains how sound waves travel through our ears?
   a. Volume 1
   b. Volume 2
   c. Volume 3
   d. Volume 7

Check your answer. You are looking for information about how the ear works. The answer is **b**.

2. Which volume would tell you if a zither is an animal, an instrument, or a jacket?
   a. Volume 8
   b. Volume 7
   c. Volume 9
   d. Volume 10

3. Which volume would tell you about Nero and other rulers of Rome?
   a. Volume 2
   b. Volume 4
   c. Volume 6
   d. Volume 8

4. Which volume would tell you about woofers, tweeters, and other parts of a stereo system?
   a. Volume 7
   b. Volume 8
   c. Volume 9
   d. Volume 10

5. "Every four years, the number of lemmings (little mouselike animals) becomes too many. The lemmings then head for the sea where most of them drown." Which volume would tell you if this story is true or false?
   a. Volume 1
   b. Volume 2
   c. Volume 3
   d. Volume 4

The 2,000-Year-Old Pizza

Roman soldiers ate pizza more than 2,000 years ago. But the first fast food place to offer pizza opened in the U.S. less than 100 years ago. New York Pizzeria opened in 1895.

Pizza used to be an Italian pie. American soldiers in Europe liked it and brought the idea home. Now pizza is as American as hot dogs and Chevrolets. In fact, the words *pizza* and *pizzeria* appear in most American dictionaries.

All the facts in the story above did not come from the same source. Some came from an encyclopedia. Others appeared in a book about fast food in America. One fact came from a dictionary. A newspaper told another fact. As you can see, the writer of the above story used many sources.

Suppose you are writing a story based on facts. First, decide what facts you need. Then choose the sources where the facts are likely to be.

Choose the best answer.

1. Where should you look to find out how to make duck soup?
   a. in a dictionary under *d*
   b. in an encyclopedia
   c. in a cookbook
   d. in a textbook

Check your answer. Duck soup is something you cook. The correct answer is **c**.

2. Which of these would most likely tell about the weather yesterday?
   a. a newspaper
   b. an almanac
   c. a science textbook
   d. a dictionary

3. Where would you be most likely to find facts about treating a burn?
   a. in a cookbook
   b. in a first-aid book
   c. in a newspaper
   d. in a telephone book

4. Which reference would you use to find Dwight Gooden's pitching record in 1985?
   a. encyclopedia
   b. textbook
   c. almanac
   d. dictionary

5. Which of these would tell you the meaning of the word *publication*?
   a. a public notice
   b. a dictionary
   c. a spelling book
   d. a newspaper

TAKING TESTS

Practice your reference skills as you follow the test-taking tips on the next three pages. Put your answers on your answer sheet.

Test Tips: Most reference materials are arranged in alphabetical order. Study skills tests often include exercises on alphabetizing.

Choose the word that would appear first if the four words or names were arranged in alphabetical order.

1. a. encyclopedia
   b. dictionary
   c. famous
   d. garlic

2. a. book
   b. almanac
   c. atlas
   d. cookbook

3. a. Cooper, Carol
   b. Crandell, Karen
   c. Cruz, Rafael
   d. Chin, Joseph

4. a. library
   b. librarian
   c. liberty
   d. license

Test Tips: Most study skills tests include questions about the purpose of each reference material. You should know where to look for certain kinds of facts.

Choose the best answer.

5. Which one of these would tell you the title of a chapter?
   a. index
   b. table of contents
   c. dictionary
   d. almanac

6. Which of these would give a list of the best-selling books of the past year?
   a. dictionary
   b. almanac
   c. telephone book
   d. encyclopedia

7. Which reference would tell you the meaning of the word *consumer*?
   a. dictionary
   b. almanac
   c. telephone book
   d. encyclopedia

8. Which of these would tell you how to pronounce the word *ukelele*?
   a. encyclopedia
   b. dictionary
   c. a music book
   d. almanac

Test Tips: Many tests include questions about a table of contents or an index. In this case, remember to read the questions first. Then find the correct answer on the index or table of contents.

Here is the table of contents of the book called *Fantastic Facts.* Use it to answer the questions below.

TABLE OF CONTENTS

Chapter	Page
1—Wheels	6
2—Leave It to Levi	10
3—A Monster from the Past	16
4—Animals' Best Friend	20
5—Something's Fishy	30
6—Upside-Down Tree	52
7—Space Shuttle	76

Choose the best answer.

1. What chapter might give information on bicycles?
   a. 1
   b. 3
   c. 5
   d. 7

2. The baobab's branches look like roots reaching for the sky. You might find more details about the baobab tree in the chapter that begins on page __.
   a. 52
   b. 53
   c. 20
   d. 21

3. Blue jeans is most likely to be a topic in chapter __.
   a. 1
   b. 2
   c. 3
   d. 4

4. Which chapter would most likely have a story of a man who smells fish to earn a living?
   a. 4
   b. 5
   c. 20
   d. 30

Here is the index of the same book, *Fantastic Facts*. Use it to answer the questions below.

INDEX

Accident, First Bike, 6
Africa, 52
Animal Talent Scouts, Inc., 20–21
Animal trainer, 20–21
Baobab tree, 52–53
Bike, 6–7
Columbia Space Shuttle, 76–77
Dracula, 16
Fish, Rotten, 30–31
Food and Drug Administration, 30
Jeans, 10–11
Stoker, Bram, 16–17
Strauss, Levi, 10–11
Tepes, Vlad, 16–17
Vampires, 16–17
Weber, Al, 30–31

Choose the best answer.

1. Which page would tell you about a person who trained an elephant?
   a. 16
   b. 30
   c. 20
   d. 52

2. Which pages would tell you about the founder of Levi's, Levi Strauss?
   a. 10–11
   b. 16–17
   c. 20–31
   d. 30–31

3. Vlad Tepes was the real Count Dracula. On which pages might you find a story about him?
   a. 20–21
   b. 52–53
   c. 6–7
   d. 16–17

4. On which pages might you find a description of a trip to the moon?
   a. 6–7
   b. 76–77
   c. 30–31
   d. 10–11

UNIT IV
TESTS

Test 1

Reading Comprehension   198
Vocabulary   202
Study Skills   205

Test 2

Reading Comprehension   208
Vocabulary   212
Study Skills   215

READING COMPREHENSION

Directions: This test will show how well you understand what you read. Read each passage. Then do the items that follow it. Choose the best answer for each item. On your answer sheet, fill in the space that goes with the answer you choose.

The Golden Gate Bridge is in San Francisco. The bridge crosses part of a bay and leads to roads going north. Until 1937, there was no bridge at this place. The only way across was by ferry boat. The space seemed too big for a bridge. But one man, Joseph B. Strauss, had always wanted to build a bridge there. Finally, he got his way.

Joseph Strauss drew up plans for the new bridge. The Golden Gate Bridge would be a suspension bridge. The roadway would hang from giant cables—thick ropes of steel. At each end of the bridge, huge towers would hold up the cables.

Work on the bridge began in 1933 and went on for four years. Workmen climbed hundreds of feet above the icy water. A net was stretched under the bridge to catch any workers who might fall. Some did fall into the net and were rescued.

Joseph Strauss's dream came true on May 28, 1937. Long lines of cars crossed the bridge for the first time on that day.

---

1. What is the best name for this story?
   a. "The Life of Joseph Strauss"
   b. "Ferry Boats of Long Ago"
   c. "How a Bridge Was Built"
   d. "The San Francisco Bay"

2. What is a suspension bridge?
   a. a very long bridge
   b. a bridge in which the roadway hangs from cables
   c. a bridge across a bay
   d. a bridge with a net under it

3. Cables on a bridge are made of ___.
   a. steel   c. string
   b. wood   d. rubber

4. The job of building the bridge must have been ___.
   a. funny
   b. dull
   c. easy
   d. dangerous

5. The Golden Gate Bridge has been open for ___.
   a. four years
   b. more than 40 years
   c. 100 years
   d. a short time

¹ You can do almost anything with kites. You can fish with them, pull boats with them, or race them. You can use a kite to study the weather, take pictures, or scare off crows. Or you can just let a kite sail in the wind.

² Kites have been around for thousands of years. In that time, people have found many uses for kites. The first kites were probably flown in China. Kites flying at night over the houses were supposed to keep evil spirits away.

³ Americans used kites to try out new ideas in science. Benjamin Franklin hung a metal key from a kite string. He showed that lightning was electricity. The Wright brothers used kites to lift themselves into the air. Later they made one of the first airplanes.

⁴ Kites are easiest to fly in open spaces. The wind should be blowing between 5 and 15 miles an hour. With less wind, it's hard to lift a kite. With too much wind, a kite is hard to handle.

---

6. What is the main idea of paragraph 1?
  a. Kites can pull boats.
  b. Kites are used in many ways.
  c. Kites can scare off crows.
  d. You can fly a kite at night.

7. The first kites were probably used in __.
  a. America   c. the water
  b. China   d. the winter

8. Which statement is true?
  a. Kites were invented in America.
  b. Benjamin Franklin made the first kite.
  c. Kites work the same way as airplanes.
  d. Kites were used against evil spirits.

9. What is paragraph 4 mostly about?
  a. how to fly a kite
  b. how to make a kite
  c. how much wind kites need
  d. how much kites cost

10. Fly a kite in an open space because __.
  a. the wind blows freely
  b. there is no wind
  c. there are more trees
  d. more people can watch

A Minor Bird

I have wished a bird would fly away,
And not sing by my house all day;

Have clapped my hands at him from the door
When it seemed as if I could bear no more.

The fault must partly have been in me.
The bird was not to blame for his key.

And of course there must be something wrong
In wanting to silence any song.

Robert Frost

---

11. Where did the bird sing?
   a. in a park
   b. in a nest
   c. near the poet's house
   d. in a cage

12. Why did the poet clap his hands?
   a. to make the bird fly away
   b. to make the bird fly in the house
   c. to make the bird take food
   d. to make the bird sing louder

13. What is the "key" in the poem?
   a. a word from a song
   b. a bird's wings
   c. something that unlocks a door
   d. the way the bird's song sounds

14. Who does the poet blame for his anger at the bird?
   a. the bird
   b. the poet himself
   c. the whole world
   d. all birds

15. Which of these ideas would the poet most likely agree with?
   a. We should sing like birds.
   b. There are too many birds.
   c. We should enjoy a bird's song.
   d. Birds can't sing well.

¹ Lake Maracaibo is a place to find buried treasure. The buried treasure is not gold or silver. It is oil. Hundreds of towers stand in the lake. They are oil derricks. The derricks bring up oil from the bottom of the lake.

² Lake Maracaibo is in Venezuela. The oil from the lake has made Venezuela the richest country in South America. Venezuela sells huge amounts of oil to other countries. But oil is the only big "crop" in Venezuela. There is not enough land to grow food for the country's people.

³ Only a tiny part of Venezuela is farmland. Forests cover one-fourth of the country. Mountains take up another big part. Venezuela has to depend on other countries for most of its food.

16. What is true about the oil in Venezuela?
   a. There is no oil in Venezuela.
   b. The oil has made Venezuela rich.
   c. Venezuela buys its oil.
   d. The oil in Venezuela is gold.

17. What is paragraph 1 mostly about?
   a. the oil in Lake Maracaibo
   b. the gold in Lake Maracaibo
   c. the land in Venezuela
   d. the countries in South America

18. Oil is a kind of "treasure" because __.
   a. it is very heavy
   b. it is in the ground
   c. it is worth a lot of money
   d. it is on a farm

19. What is paragraph 3 mostly about?
   a. the amount of oil in Venezuela
   b. the number of farmers in Venezuela
   c. how Venezuela got its name
   d. the kind of land in Venezuela

20. Where does Venezuela get most of its food?
   a. from farmers in Venezuela
   b. from farmers in other countries
   c. from forests and mountains
   d. from Lake Maracaibo

VOCABULARY

Directions: This test will show if you can recognize words that have the same meaning, words that have opposite meanings, words that sound alike, and words with several meanings. Mark your answers on your answer sheet.

For items 1–8 choose the word or phrase that means the same, or almost the same, as the word in dark type.

1. **Directing** the way
   a. finding
   b. leading
   c. knowing
   d. following

2. Find **assistance**
   a. friends
   b. treasure
   c. a sister
   d. help

3. Feel **discomfort**
   a. comfortable
   b. soft
   c. pain
   d. angry

4. **Originated** the story
   a. wrote
   b. heard
   c. knew
   d. began

5. **Partially** broken
   a. partly
   b. painfully
   c. completely
   d. accidentally

6. An **ordinary** day
   a. not special
   b. unusual
   c. wonderful
   d. cold

7. **Perished** suddenly
   a. spoke
   b. died
   c. laughed
   d. yelled

8. A **restless** person
   a. happy
   b. kind
   c. lazy
   d. unrelaxed

For items 9–16 choose the word or phrase that means the opposite of the word in dark type.

9. **Purchase** a house
   a. buy
   b. furnish
   c. sell
   d. leave

10. A **risky** act
    a. true
    b. dangerous
    c. safe
    d. rash

11. **Settle** in town
    a. move
    b. stay
    c. live
    d. shop

12. **Ascend** the stairs
    a. go up
    b. walk on
    c. fall on
    d. go down

13. A **mountainous** area
    a. high
    b. flat
    c. beautiful
    d. ugly

14. Be **honorable**
    a. respectful
    b. honest
    c. unlawful
    d. unlovable

15. A **valuable** ring
    a. large
    b. rich
    c. profitable
    d. worthless

16. Was **displeased** about
    a. lonely
    b. wrong
    c. happy
    d. angry

For items 17–22 choose the sentence in which the word in dark type means the same as the definition given.

17. all by itself
    a. A dress was the **lone** thing in Helen's bag.
    b. The man needed a bank **loan**.
    c. I got a book on **loan**.

18. pushed or drilled
    a. I was **bored** at the party.
    b. The workman **bored** a small hole.
    c. I used an oak **board** as a shelf.

19. joined in
    a. Alice **entered** the room late.
    b. I saw her when I **entered** the school.
    c. Have you **entered** the contest yet?

20. mark a line
    a. the gang had a secret **plot**.
    b. George will **plot** the route of the trip.
    c. The story had an interesting **plot**.

21. presented a story
    a. Are those two words **related**?
    b. Steve is not **related** to Anne.
    c. Otto **related** the details of the trip.

22. hung something up
    a. Rob was **suspended** from school.
    b. Arnie **suspended** the shelf from the wall.
    c. The football game was **suspended**.

STUDY SKILLS

Directions: This test will show how well you can get and use information from maps, graphs, tables, and reference materials. Read each question. Four answers are given, but only one is right. On your answer sheet, fill in the space for the best answer.

MAY

SUN.	MON.	TUES.	WED.	THURS.	FRI.	SAT.
1	2	3	4	5	6	7
8	9	10	11	12	13	14
15	16	17	18	19	20	21
22	23	24	25	26	27	28
29	30	31				

1. Mother's Day is on May 8. What day of the week is it?
   a. Sunday   c. Thursday
   b. Tuesday   d. Saturday

2. Memorial Day is the last Monday in May. What date is that?
   a. the 23rd   c. the 30th
   b. the 24th   d. the 31st

3. On May 11, Carl took his jacket to the cleaners. He was told that it would be ready in a week. What date would that be?
   a. the 17th   c. the 19th
   b. the 18th   d. the 20th

4. Which capital city is shown on the map?
   a. Dallas   c. Houston
   b. Fort Worth   d. Austin

5. Which river divides Texas and Mexico?
   a. Colorado   c. Rio Grande
   b. Trinity   d. San Antonio

6. What direction would you take to get from Austin to Forth Worth?
   a. north   c. east
   b. south   d. west

7. Which state borders Texas in the northwest?
   a. Oklahoma   c. Arkansas
   b. New Mexico   d. Louisiana

205

NUMBER OF BABIES BORN IN THE U.S., 1955-1985

(IN MILLIONS)

4.2 —	
4.0 —	
3.8 —	
3.6 —	
3.4 —	
3.2 —	
3.0 —	

1955 1960 1965 1970 1975 1980 1985

EARTHQUAKES

Date	Location	Deaths (Est.)
1970	Peru	66,794
1976	China	655,235
1978	Japan	21
1978	Iran	25,000
1985	Mexico	10,000

8. This graph shows __.
   a. why few U.S babies were born in 1975
   b. how many babies were born in each U.S. family
   c. how many babies were born in the U.S. in certain years
   d. that the U.S. population is growing

9. The year on the graph when the most U.S. babies were born is __.
   a. 1955   c. 1965
   b. 1960   d. 1980

10. In 1965, the number of babies born in the U.S. was __.
    a. 3.8   c. 3,600
    b. 3,600,000   d. 3,800,000

11. The one nation that suffered the highest death toll in earthquakes was __ .
    a. China   c. Mexico
    b. Peru   d. Iran

12. Another title for this table might be __.
    a. Deaths in Five Countries
    b. Earthquakes in Europe
    c. When Earthquakes Happened
    d. Deaths in Recent Earthquakes

13. In what year were there two earthquakes?
    a. 1970   c. 1978
    b. 1976   d. 1980

14. Where was the most recent earthquake on this table?
    a. Peru   c. Japan
    b. China   d. Mexico

INDEX FROM AN ALMANAC

Actors and Actresses 385–399
Automobiles 123–125
Books .426
Cities 194–197
Crime 966–969
Disasters 748–755
Energy 249–250
Food 133–148
History 706–747
Holidays 792–794
Laws 466–477
News .36
Space Flights 126–132
Sports 818–913
States 678–702
Television 429–431
U.S. Facts 456–466
Weather 795–802
Women 247–248

15. On what pages would you find facts about baseball?
    a. 426–431   c. 429–431
    b. 818–913   d. 456–466

16. Which pages would tell you about the new laws that were passed last year?
    a. 466–477   c. 249–250
    b. 966–969   d. 247–248

17. If *Environment* were added to this index, where would it appear?
    a. before *Disasters*
    b. between *Disasters* and *Energy*
    c. after *Energy*
    d. between *Food* and *History*

18. Where would you look to find out when Gary Coleman was born?
    a. in a dictionary
    b. in an atlas
    c. in an almanac
    d. in an encyclopedia

19. Which one of these would most likely tell about yesterday's parade?
    a. a newspaper
    b. a book about parades
    c. a city map
    d. a magazine

20. Which source would you use to find out everything you need to know about jazz?
    a. dictionary
    b. atlas
    c. almanac
    d. encyclopedia

21. Where would you be most likely to find an alphabetical listing of people who live in a city?
    a. dictionary
    b. telephone book
    c. library
    d. almanac

22. Which one of these would tell you what Chapter 2 is all about?
    a. index
    b. table of contents
    c. card catalog
    d. pronunciation key

READING COMPREHENSION

Directions: This test offers several reading selections. Read each selection and then answer the questions. Four answers are given for each exercise, but only one of these answers is right. On your answer sheet, fill in the space that goes with the answer you choose.

In late summer, many storms start in the Atlantic Ocean. Some of these storms become hurricanes. Hurricanes happen when the air is warmest. Warm air rises from the water and mixes with cool air. Rain, thunder, and lightning break out. The winds get stronger. Winds in a hurricane can blow as fast as 200 miles an hour.

Many times, hurricanes have hit hard along the coasts of U.S. southern states. People in Gulfport, Mississippi, will never forget the hurricane of August, 1969. This hurricane killed more than 100 people. The storm was the strongest that had ever hit the U.S. coast.

Years ago, hurricanes took people by surprise. Now scientists can tell ahead of time how strong a hurricane will be. Radio programs carry news about the storms. Warning flags go up near the coast. People along the coast can plan ways to keep safe.

1. At what time of year do hurricanes first break out?
   a. in spring
   b. in late summer
   c. in late fall
   d. in winter

2. A hurricane is different from a small storm because it has __.
   a. warmer air
   b. cooler air
   c. stronger winds
   d. no winds

3. Hurricanes don't start in cold weather because __.
   a. there is too much rain
   b. the ocean water is too deep
   c. the winds blow too fast
   d. the ocean water is too cold

4. People can find out quickly about a new hurricane by __.
   a. listening to the radio
   b. writing to scientists
   c. going to Gulfport
   d. flying a flag

5. What is the last paragraph of the article about?
   a. how hurricanes start
   b. getting news about a hurricane
   c. the winds of a hurricane
   d. a hurricane in Gulfport

How would you like a trip to the moon? Men have already landed there. Someday, the moon might be a popular place to visit. What would a trip to the moon be like? Here are some facts.

There is no air or water on the moon. To stay alive, you would have to take your own oxygen and your own supply of water. It is silent on the moon because there is no air. Sounds can't be carried from place to place. At night, the temperature goes down to 240° F below zero. During the day, the moon warms up—to 212° F above zero.

What will the surface of the moon look like? The moon has great round holes in it. There are more than 30,000 of these holes. One of the biggest is 146 miles across.

When you walk on the moon, you'll feel light on your feet. That's because you will weigh only one-sixth as much as you do on Earth. A 120-pound person will weigh only about 20 pounds on the moon.

You might forget what day it is on the moon because a moon day lasts for two weeks. But at least you won't need a raincoat. It never rains on the moon. The weather on the moon never changes at all.

6. Which of the following is a true statement about the moon?
   a. The moon has clean air.
   b. Some people live on the moon.
   c. There is no water on the moon.
   d. The moon is always cold.

7. The best title for this selection is ___.
   a. "What the Moon Is Like"
   b. "The Weather on the Moon"
   c. "How to Go to the Moon"
   d. "The Moon People"

8. At night the temperature on the moon is ___.
   a. 212° F above zero
   b. the same as it is on Earth
   c. higher than it is on Earth
   d. lower than it is on Earth

9. What is true about the surface of the moon?
   a. It has roads.
   b. It has many holes.
   c. It is wet.
   d. It is smooth.

10. A day on the moon lasts as long as ___.
   a. a day on Earth
   b. a week on Earth
   c. two weeks on Earth
   d. a year on Earth

Your feet take a lot of wear and tear. Most people walk over 100,000 miles in a lifetime. That's like walking four times around the earth. No wonder our feet get tired! Four out of five Americans have foot problems, some doctors say. The shoes we wear cause some of these problems.

Heels on women's shoes are on the rise. That is why some women have foot problems. Shoes with high heels and narrow toes can harm the feet. High heels pull the body forward with each step. After a while, the bones in the feet may begin to bend. The feet may really start to hurt.

What kinds of shoes are best for the feet? Shoes should have low heels, and the soles should not be too thin. A shoe should be at least half an inch longer than your longest toe. Sneakers and sandals should be as well made as other kinds of shoes.

---

11. This selection is mostly about __.
    a. bones in the feet
    b. walking around the world
    c. our foot problems
    d. sneakers and sandals

12. About how many Americans have foot problems?
    a. forty-five
    b. four out of five
    c. one hundred thousand
    d. one million

13. Many foot problems are caused by __.
    a. walking too much
    b. sneakers and sandals
    c. wearing high heels
    d. sore feet

14. Which of these is the best title for this selection?
    a. "Be Good to Your Feet"
    b. "The Longest Walk"
    c. "The High Cost of High Heels"
    d. "New Shoe Styles"

15. A shoe that fits the best is __.
    a. just as long as your foot
    b. longer than your heel
    c. narrow in the toe
    d. longer than your longest toe

The following is part of a day-by-day log. A teenage boy wrote the log while on a Navy ship headed for Greenland.

JUNE 28: Today we saw land for the first time since the ship left port. I went to the ship's bridge to find out where we were. We were about 25 miles south of Nova Scotia. Later, I watched our first "man-overboard" drill. A life ring was thrown overboard. Some crewmen went out in a lifeboat and "rescued" the ring.

JUNE 30: I woke up to the sound of a ship's mate shouting "Icebergs!" I saw my first iceberg, but there were many more to come. Ships have to watch out for icebergs. They can cut a hole in steel in minutes.

JULY 3: I heard I would get my first look at Greenland today. The ship came near the coast. Everyone was quiet and tense. We were passing near some dangerous rocks. Then we all breathed a sigh of relief. The ship passed between the cliffs on Greenland's coast. Up ahead, snow-covered mountains reached to the clouds. Greenland!

16. What is this passage mainly about?
   a. a lifeboat drill
   b. how icebergs put ships in danger
   c. the people of Greenland
   d. a trip to Greenland by ship

17. On June 28 the ship was __.
   a. near Greenland
   b. near Nova Scotia
   c. in a port
   d. on an iceberg

18. Why did the crew "rescue" a life ring?
   a. to show how a person could be rescued
   b. to show how to swim
   c. to search for a lifeboat
   d. to find an iceberg

19. Ships must watch out for icebergs because __.
   a. icebergs can sink
   b. icebergs are under a bridge
   c. icebergs cannot be seen
   d. icebergs can make a hole in a ship

20. At the end of the passage, the writer feels __.
   a. afraid
   b. angry
   c. relieved
   d. tired

VOCABULARY

Directions: This test will show if you understand the meaning of different words and if you recognize words that have the same meaning. Mark your answers on your answer sheet.

For items 1–8, choose the word or phrase that means the same, or almost the same, as the word in dark type.

1. **Guide** someone home
   a. lose
   b. lead
   c. follow
   d. drive

2. Strong **emotions**
   a. ideas
   b. moves
   c. muscles
   d. feelings

3. A **bare** shelf
   a. empty
   b. wood
   c. large
   d. hard

4. **Communicate** with someone
   a. fight
   b. talk
   c. walk
   d. go to church

5. **Astounded** his friends
   a. met
   b. talked with
   c. followed
   d. surprised

6. Look for a **remedy**
   a. cure
   b. person
   c. doctor
   d. book

7. A **profitable** idea
   a. money-making
   b. future
   c. smart
   d. strange

8. **Considerably** different
   a. partly
   b. nicely
   c. very
   d. not much

For items 9–16 read each sentence beginning. Choose the word or phrase that best completes each sentence.

9. A bird that is aloft is __.
a. on the ground
b. in the air
c. lost
d. laying an egg

10. A gale is a kind of __.
a. storm
b. stick
c. window
d. sickness

11. People who are in a panic are __.
a. happy
b. rich
c. alarmed
d. tired

12. If something is propelled, it is __.
a. expensive
b. very small
c. sick
d. pushed forward

13. You should halt at a __.
a. green light
b. festival
c. stop sign
d. car race

14. An archaeologist studies __.
a. arithmetic
b. bugs
c. the weather
d. ancient things

15. Another word for accomplishment is __.
a. building
b. feat
c. heir
d. journey

16. A requirement is something you __.
a. hope for
b. hate
c. must do
d. are afraid of

For items 17–22, read the selection below. Notice the words in dark type. Choose the word or phrase that best answers each question about the words in dark type.

Death Valley in California has a scary name. Very few people die there now. But in 1849, many people did **perish** in the valley. That is how it got its name.

In 1849, 30 people were going to California to look for gold. They had to pass through a valley. The weather in the valley was very hot during the day but **freezing** during the night. It was also very dry.

The travelers became lost in the valley. Soon they **exhausted** all of their water. Their throats became **parched**. They looked for water to wet their dry throats. The water they found was filled with **poisonous** chemicals. They knew that drinking the water could kill them.

Most of the travelers died in the valley. The ones who **survived**, stayed alive, called the place "Death Valley." The name stuck.

17. What does **perish** mean in the selection?
    a. find
    b. scare
    c. die
    d. name

18. What does **freezing** mean in the selection?
    a. cold
    b. hot
    c. dry
    d. pretty

19. What does **exhausted** mean in the selection?
    a. tired
    b. wet
    c. lost
    d. used up

20. What does **parched** mean in the selection?
    a. dead
    b. dry
    c. wet
    d. unhappy

21. What does **poisonous** mean in the selection?
    a. deadly
    b. sweet
    c. dry
    d. water

22. What does **survived** mean in the selection
    a. die
    b. find gold
    c. stayed alive
    d. drink

STUDY SKILLS

Directions: This test will show how well you can get and use information from maps, tables, graphs, and reference materials. Read each question. Four answers are given, but only one is right. On your sheet, fill in the space for the best answer.

DEPARTURES			
Flight	**To**	**Gate**	**Time**
AA 124	Boston	3	7:00a.m.
TW 193	Chicago	12	7:45a.m.
UA 701	Denver	7	8:00a.m.
EA 195	Miami	4	11:47a.m.
DL 707	Atlanta	11	12:00N

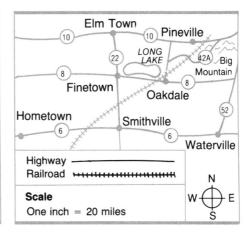

Highway ———
Railroad ╫╫╫╫╫╫╫╫╫╫╫╫╫╫╫

Scale
One inch = 20 miles

1. Where would you most likely find the above table?
   a. library   c. school
   b. airport   d. boat dock

2. What time does the plane for Chicago leave?
   a. 7:00 a.m.   c. 7:45 a.m.
   b. 8:00 a.m.   d. 11:47 a.m.

3. From which gate does DL 707 leave?
   a. 12   c. 4
   b. 7   d. 11

4. Which flight goes to Denver?
   a. AA 124   c. UA 701
   b. TW 193   d. EA 195

5. On the above map, Elm Town is __ of Finetown.
   a. north   c. east
   b. south   d. west

6. The train from Pineville to Oakdale goes in what direction?
   a. northeast
   b. northwest
   c. southeast
   d. southwest

7. Smithville is 20 miles east of __.
   a. Hometown   c. Pineville
   b. Finetown   d. Oakdale

8. Which routes would you use to get from Smithville to Big Mountain?
   a. 22, 10   c. 8, 42A
   b. 6, 22   d. 6, 8

215

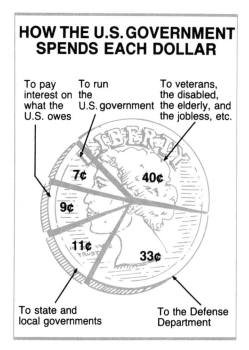

HOW THE U.S. GOVERNMENT SPENDS EACH DOLLAR

To pay interest on what the U.S. owes

To run the U.S. government

To veterans, the disabled, the elderly, and the jobless, etc.

7¢

40¢

9¢

11¢

33¢

To state and local governments

To the Defense Department

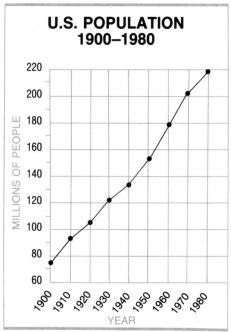

U.S. POPULATION 1900–1980

MILLIONS OF PEOPLE

YEAR

9. The U.S. spends the least money on ___.
   a. running the government
   b. helping the states
   c. keeping the U.S. army
   d. paying for interest

10. The biggest expense for the U.S. government is for ___.
    a. defense
    b. state and local aid
    c. helping the needy
    d. running the White House

11. How much of every tax dollar does the U.S. give to the state and local governments?
    a. 7¢   c. 11¢
    b. 9¢   d. 40¢

12. What change has happened to the U.S. population from 1900 to 1980?
    a. It has remained the same.
    b. It increased greatly.
    c. The number of people dropped.
    d. It was up and down.

13. In what period was the growth in population slowest?
    a. 1900–1910   c. 1930–1940
    b. 1920–1930   d. 1960–1970

14. In what period did the U.S. population increase the most?
    a. 1930–1940   c. 1900–1910
    b. 1950–1960   d. 1970–1980

15. In 1970, about how many people lived in the U.S.?
    a. 200   c. 2,000,000
    b. 200,000   d. 200,000,000

216

ALMANAC — GENERAL INDEX

Cities, U.S.—   637–701

Area codes, telephone . 771–772
Buildings, tall 671–676
Crime 153
Income tax 117
Libraries, public 268
Mayors 83–86
Mileage tables 203–215
Newspapers 410–411
Police 155
Population 933–957
Sports 837–847
Time differences 790
Weather 417–421
Zip Codes 204–228

16. On what pages would you find a list of tall buildings?
    a. 771–772   c. 203–215
    b. 671–676   d. 410–411

17. Which pages would tell you about football teams in U.S. cities?
    a. 410–411   c. 933–957
    b. 837–847   d. 417–421

18. If *Food* were added to this index, where would it appear?
    a. between *Crime* and *Income tax*
    b. after *Buildings*
    c. between *Libraries* and *Mayors*
    d. before *Crime*

19. Which lists topics alphabetically in a book?
    a. table of contents
    b. key or legend
    c. index
    d. volume

20. Which would most likely show how many islands there are in Hawaii?
    a. atlas
    b. dictionary
    c. encyclopedia
    d. almanac

21. What is the best source for facts about dinosaurs?
    a. atlas
    b. dictionary
    c. encyclopedia
    d. almanac

22. Where would you look to find out how to make butter cookies?
    a. in a telephone book
    b. in a newspaper
    c. in a card catalog
    d. in a cookbook

23. Which of these would help you learn to use the word *project* correctly?
    a. a language book
    b. a newspaper
    c. a dictionary
    d. a movie guide

Vocabulary Glossary

Here are all of the new words and their meanings which you learned in the different lessons. Remember, sometimes a word can have more than one meaning. The meanings listed here fit the way the words were used in the stories.

accept — believe or agree with

accompanied — went together with

accomplishment — something important a person did

addition — something added

aloft — high up in the air

amazing — surprising

ancient — very old

archaeologist — person who studies old things

area — a place

ascend — climb up

assist — help

astounded — very surprised

attack — start a fight with

authorities — people in charge

banner — very good

bare — empty or not covered

base — bottom of something

bored — pushed or drilled

bulky — thick

capture — take

cargo — things carried by boats

cleanliness — clean conditions

collect — save

communicate — talk

competition — people or teams which play against others

composer — writer of music

concert — musical performance

considerably — very much

constructed — made up

contest — a game that someone wins

conversations — talks

convict — find guilty

craft — boat or airplane

crew — a team of people who work together

current — a movement of air or water

currently — at the present time

cutter — a small, fast boat

damage — do harm to something

depressed — unhappy

destroy — tear up

difficulty — a problem or trouble

discomfort — an uncomfortable or painful feeling

displeased — angry

earliest — the first

elevated — lifted up or raised

emotions — feelings

employed — having a job

enormous — very large

entered — joined in

escape — get away from danger

escorted — went with

especially — in a very good or special way

events — things that happen

exhausted — tired or used up

expensive — costly

experience — feel or live through something

explorers — people who travel to new places

exterminated — killed

feat — accomplishment or deed

females — women or girls

festival — a big party or fair

floor — all parts of a building at the same height

furnish — give or provide

gale — a storm with strong winds

growth — becoming bigger

guessed — made an answer without knowing for sure

guide — lead to a place

halted — brought to a stop

heir — person who is left something by someone who has died

homeland — birthplace

honorable — doing the right thing

injured — hurt or harmed

instruct — teach

invented — made something before anyone else

issued — sent out

journeyed — made a trip

limit — the top point that you are allowed to reach

livelihood — way of making money to live

locate — find out where something is

lone — all by itself

maestro — master of an art

mountainous — having many mountains

national — belonging to a whole country

newcomers — people who come to a new place

object — a goal or purpose

observed — saw something happen

occur — happen

operate — use or run

opponents — people whom you play against

ordinary — not special

organization — a group or club

originated — was invented or started

overcame — won over or beat

overnight — in just one night or quickly

partially — part of

passport — document used for travel

perished — died

physician — a person who treats sick people

piece — one part of something

plot — mark a line on a map

preserved — kept in good shape

pressure — a weight that pushes against something else

profitable — money-making

propelled — pushed or moved forward

purchase — buy

rapid — fast or quick

rare — unusual

recent — new or up-to-date

records — information put down in writing

recover — get well

reflects — throws or sends back

relieved — made something easier

remedy — something that cures a sickness

requirement — something you need to do

restless — not able to rest or relax

risky — dangerous

role — part

root — cheer or want someone to win

scene — spot where something happens

scheduled — planned ahead of time

security — protection

seller — someone who trades something for money

settle — live in one place

shortage — amount that is not enough

site — a place where something is located

skyscrapers — very tall buildings

soil — ground or dirt

solution — an answer

spectator — one who watches

sponsored — organized

star — very good actor or athlete

stare — look hard

steers — male cattle

struck— happened or hit

structure — a building

succeed — to be able to do something well and not fail

suffering — having feelings of pain

superior — very good or best

supply — something which is stored up to be used later

suspended — hung something above the ground

switch — something that turns a machine on or off

term — word

their — belonging to them

through — from one side to the other

tomb — burying place

toss — throw something

totally — completely

tradition — old beliefs

transmit — send from one place to another

underneath — below

unfortunate — unlucky

valuable — worth a lot

vicious — very mean or dangerous

victory — a win

voyages — trips made on boats

wealth — riches

weight— how heavy something is

whether — if

whole — all of something

write — put words on paper

Answer Key

UNIT I   READING COMPREHENSION

Pages 8–9:   1. c, 2. b, 3. a, 4. c, 5. b
Pages 10–11:   1. b, 2. b, 3. c, 4. a, 5. c
Pages 12–13:   1. b, 2. b, 3. a, **4. b, 5. b**
Pages 14–15:   1. a, 2. c, 3. a, 4. b, 5. b
Pages 16–17:   1. c, 2. a, 3. c, 4. b, 5. c
Pages 18–19:   1. a, 2. b, 3. a, 4. b, 5. c
Pages 20–21:   1. b, 2. c, 3. a, 4. b, 5. a
Pages 22–23:   1. c, 2. a, 3. b, 4. a, 5. b
Page 24:   1. b, 2. a, 3. c, 4. d, 5. b
Page 25:   1. a, 2. b, 3. c, 4. a, 5. c
Page 26:   1. d, 2. c, 3. a, 4. c, 5. b
Page 27:   1. b, 2. c, 3. a, 4. c, 5. d
Pages 28–29:   1. c, 2. b, 3. a, 4. b, 5. c
Pages 30–31:   1. a, 2. c, 3. b, 4. c, 5. c
Pages 32–33:   1. b, 2. a, 3. b, 4. c, 5. a
Pages 34–35:   1. b, 2. a, 3. b, 4. b, 5. c
Pages 36–37:   1. c, 2. b, 3. a, 4. a, 5. c
Pages 38–39:   1. b, 2. a, 3. b, 4. c, 5. a
Pages 40–41:   1. c, 2. b, 3. a, 4. a, 5. c
Pages 42–43:   1. c, 2. b, 3. a, 4. c, 5. b
Pages 44–45:   1. a, 2. c, 3. b, 4. b, 5. c
Page 46:   1. c, 2. b, 3. a, 4. b, 5. d
Page 47:   1. a, 2. c, 3. d, 4. b, 5. c
Page 48:   **1. b, 2. b, 3. c, 4. d, 5. a**
Page 49:   1. c, 2. b, 3. a, 4. c, 5. d
Pages 50–51:   1. b, 2. b, 3. a, 4. b, 5. c
Pages 52–53:   1. c, 2. a, 3. b, 4. b, 5. c
Pages 54–55:   1. a, 2. c, 3. a, 4. c, 5. b
Pages 56–57:   1. a, 2. c, 3. b, 4. a, 5. b
Pages 58–59:   1. b, 2. b, 3. c, 4. b, 5. c
Pages 60–61:   1. a, 2. b, 3. c, 4. b, 5. b
Pages 62–63:   1. b, 2. a, 3. b, 4. c, 5. c
Pages 64–65:   1. a, 2. b, 3. b, 4. c, 5. b
Pages 66–67:   1. a, 2. b, 3. c, 4. c, 5. a
Pages 68–69:   1. b, 2. c, 3. b, 4. a, 5. c
Pages 70–71:   1. c, 2. a, 3. b, **4. a**
Pages 72–73:   1. c, 2. c, 3. a, 4. c, 5. b
Pages 74–75:   1. a, 2. c, 3. b, 4. c, 5. b
Page 76:   1. d, 2. c, 3. b, 4. b, 5. a
Page 77:   1. b, 2. a, 3. d, 4. b, 5. c
Page 78:   1. b, 2. a, 3. d, 4. b, 5. c

UNIT II VOCABULARY

Pages 84–85: **A.** 1. transmit, 2. aloft, 3. limit, 4. halted, 5. accomplishment, 6. observed, 7. invented, 8. employed; **B.** 1. b, 2. c, 3. a, 4. b

Pages 86–87: **A.** 1. requirement, 2. festival, 3. contest, 4. organization, 5. currently, 6. females, 7. events, 8. difficulty; **B.** 1. b, 2. a, 3. b, 4. c

Pages 88-89: **A.** 1. maestro, 2. sponsored, 3. concerts, 4. homeland, 5. authorities, 6. composer, 7. passport, 8. spectators; **B.** 1. c, 2. b, 3. b, 4. a

Pages 90–91: **A.** 1. journeyed, 2. settle, 3. records, 4. voyages, 5. crew, 6. soil, 7. recent, 8. explorers; **B.** 1. b, 2. c, 3. a, 4. c

Pages 92–93: **A.** 1. physician, 2. pressure, 3. remove, 4. discomfort, 5. suffering, 6. remedy, 7. bulky, 8. relieved; **B.** 1. a, 2. c, 3. b, 4. b

Pages 96–97: **A.** 1. escape, 2. unfortunate, 3. guide, 4. attack, 5. enormous, 6. vicious, 7. damage, 8. locate; **B.** 1. c, 2. b, 3. a, 4. b

Pages 98–99: **A.** 1. rapid, 2. considerably, 3. restless, 4. originated, 5. toss, 6. suspended, 7. ascend, 8. succeed; **B.** 1. a, 2. b, 3. b, 4. a

Pages 100–101: **A.** 1. totally, 2. elevated, 3. opponents, 4. injured, 5. astounded, 6. scheduled, 7. victory, 8. propelled; **B.** 1. b, 2. b, 3. c, 4. b

Pages 104–105: **A.** 1. whether, 2. whole, 3. through, 4. lone, 5. guessed, 6. bare, 7. feat, 8. stare; **B.** 1. a, 2. b, 3. a, 4. b

Pages 106–107: **A.** 1. heir, 2. weight, 3. site, 4. bored, 5. seller, 6. piece, 7. their, 8. write; **B.** 1. a, 2. a, 3. b, 4. a

Page 108: 1. b, 2. c, 3. b, 4. a, 5. d, 6. a, 7. c, 8. b

Page 109: 1. d, 2. b, 3. a, 4. b, 5. a, 6. b, 7. d, 8. b

Page 110: 1. a, 2. c, 3. b, 4. a, 5. c, 6. a, 7. b, 8. a

Page 111: 1. a, 2. b, 3. c, 4. b, 5. a, 6. b

Pages 116–117: **A.** 1. a, 2. b, 3. b, 4. c, 5. a, 6. a, 7. c, 8. a

Pages 118–119: **A.** 1. c, 2. a, 3. b, 4. c, 5. a, 6. b, 7. b, 8. c

Pages 120–121: **A.** 1. b, 2. a, 3. c, 4. a, 5. b, 6. c, 7. a, 8. b

Pages 122–123: **A.** 1. b, 2. b, 3. c, 4. a, 5. b, 6. a, 7. a, 8. c

Pages 124–125: **A.** 1. b, 2. c, 3. a, 4. b, 5. c, 6. b, 7. a, 8. c

Page 126: 1. c, 2. a, 3. d, 4. d, 5. a, 6. d, 7. c, 8. b

Page 127: 1. b, 2. c, 3. d, 4. a, 5. d, 6. b, 7. d, 8. d

Pages 132–133: **A.** 1. a, 2. b, 3. a, 4. b, 5. b, 6. a, 7. b, 8. b; **B.** 1. object, 2. craft, 3. area, 4. base

Pages 134–135: **A.** 1. b, 2. b, 3. a, 4. a, 5. b, 6. b, 7. a, 8. a; **B.** 1. struck, 2. accept, 3. steers, 4. banner

Pages 136–137: **A.** 1. a, 2. b, 3. b, 4. b, 5. a, 6. b, 7. b, 8. a; **B.** 1. solution, 2. reflects, 3. operate, 4. structure

Page 138: 1. c, 2. a, 3. b, 4. d, 5. a, 6. c, 7. c, 8. b

Page 139: 1. a, 2. b, 3. c, 4. a, 5. b, 6. c

Pages 144–145: **A.** 1. a, 2. b, 3. b, 4. a, 5. c, 6. b, 7. b, 8. c

Pages 146–147: **A.** 1. a, 2. a, 3. b, 4. c, 5. b, 6. a, 7. c, 8. b

Page 148: 1. a, 2. b, 3. d, 4. b, 5. c, 6. b

UNIT III   STUDY SKILLS

Page 151:   1. a, 2. b
Page 153:   1. c, 2. d, 3. c, 4. a, 5. c
Page 155:   1. c, 2. b, 3. d, 4. b, 5. c
Page 157:   1. a, 2. c, 3. d, 4. a, 5. b
Page 159:   1. b, 2. d, 3. c, 4. a, 5. c
Page 161:   1. a, 2. d, 3. b, 4. d, 5. c
Page 163:   1. c, 2. b, 3. d, 4. d, 5. a
Page 165:   1. a, 2. b, 3. b, 4. a, 5. d
Page 167:   1. b, 2. d, 3. b, 4. a, 5. d
Page 169:   1. c, 2. a, 3. a, 4. c, 5. b
Page 171:   1. b, 2. b, 3. a, 4. c, 5. d
Page 172:   1. c, 2. b, 3. c, 4. a, 5. a, 6. c, 7. b
Page 173:   1. d, 2. a, 3. a, 4. b, 5. d, 6. c
Page 175:   1. a, 2. d
Page 177:   1. b, 2. d, 3. d, 4. a, 5. Answers will vary.
Page 179:   1. c, 2. d, 3. c, 4. b, 5. c
Page 181:   1. b, 2. a, 3. b, 4. c, 5. b
Page 183:   1. a, 2. b, 3. a, 4. b, 5. d
Page 185:   1. c, 2. c, 3. b, 4. b, 5. a
Page 187:   1. c, 2. a, 3. c, 4. b, 5. a
Page 189:   1. a, 2. c, 3. b, 4. d, 5. a
Page 191:   1. b, 2. d, 3. c, 4. a, 5. d
Page 193:   1. c, 2. a, 3. b, 4. c, 5. b
Page 194:   1. b, 2. b, 3. d, 4. c, 5. b, 6. b, 7. a, 8. b
Page 195:   1. a, 2. a, 3. b, 4. b
Page 196:   1. c, 2. a, 3. d, 4. b

UNIT IV   TESTS

Test 1

Reading Comprehension (pages 198–201):   1. c, 2. b, 3. a, 4. d, 5. b, 6. b, 7. b, 8. d, 9. c, 10. a, 11. c, 12. a, 13. d, 14. b, 15. c, 16. b, 17. a, 18. c, 19. d, 20. b

Vocabulary (pages 202–204):   1. b, 2. d, 3. c, 4. d, 5. a, 6. a, 7. b, 8. d, 9. c, 10. c, 11. a, 12. d, 13. b, 14. c, 15. d, 16. c, 17. a, 18. b, 19. c, 20. b, 21. c, 22. b

Study Skills (pages 205–207):   1. a, 2. c, 3. b, 4. d, 5. c, 6. a, 7. b, 8. c, 9. b, 10. d, 11. a, 12. d, 13. c, 14. d, 15. b, 16. a, 17. c, 18. c, 19. a, 20. d, 21. b, 22. b

Test 2

Reading Comprehension (pages 208–211):   1. b, 2. c, 3. d, 4. a, 5. b, 6. c, 7. a, 8. d, 9. b, 10. c, 11. c, 12. b, 13. c, 14. a, 15. d, 16. d, 17. b, 18. a, 19. d, 20. c

Vocabulary (pages 212–214):   1. b, 2. d, 3. a, 4. b, 5. d, 6. a, 7. a, 8. c, 9. b, 10. a, 11. c, 12. d, 13. c, 14. d, 15. b, 16. c, 17. c, 18. a, 19. a, 20. b, 21. a, 22. c

Study Skills (pages 215–217):   1. b, 2. c, 3. d, 4. c, 5. a, 6. d, 7. a, 8. a, 9. a, 10. c, 11. c, 12. b, 13. c, 14. b, 15. d, 16. b, 17. b, 18. a, 19. c, 20. a, 21. c, 22. d, 23. c

Project Achievement: Reading—Book A